Rice

**Explorations Into
Gay Asian
Culture + Politics**

*Edited With An
Introduction By
Song Cho*

Queer Press
Toronto

Queer Press, P.O. Box 485, Station P, Toronto, Ontario, M5S 2T1

Canadian Cataloguing in Publication Data
Main entry under title:
Rice: explorations into gay Asian culture & politics
      ISBN 1-899564-05-0
1. Asian Canadian gays — Literary collections. 2. Asian American gays — Literary collections.
3. Gay men's writings, Canadian (English).* 4. Gay men's writings, American. 5. Canadian
Literature (English) — Asian Canadian authors.* 6. American Literature — Asian American
authors. 7. Canadian literature (English)—20th century. 8. American literature — 20th century
I. Cho, Song
PS8235.G38R53 1997   810.8'035206642   C97-932400-9
PR9194.5.G38R53 1997

Design by Kevin Louis Design, Vancouver
Cover photograph: Vincente Golveo & Nguyen Tan Hoang
Back photograph: Vincente Golveo
Printed and bound in Canada

Contents

VINCENTE GOLVEO

Loneliness is not so much the absence of others but far more

living among others who do not understand what you are saying

INTRODUCTION

SONG CHO

Coming out. Searching for visibility.

Rice. A life-sustaining staple of Asian cultures for thousands of years that's served as a side-dish on Western menus. Rice is also a metaphor for gay Asians and how we are consumed by a white gay culture as exotic "tricks." The term rice queen, for example, refers to white men who fetishize Asian men. This book is about reclaiming and reconnecting with this life-sustaining food as a metaphor for our culture.

Rice has many powerful resonances tied to culture and consumption. Sticky, fried or Uncle Ben's, the metaphor of rice conveys the myriad of ways we're transformed in our interaction with a white-dominant culture often to the point where we are unrecognizable even to ourselves.

Rice also conveys the idea of sexual interaction as a form of consumption, of the image and fantasy of the "Orient" that has animated Western colonialism and imperialism for the past several hundred years. Whether it's the fantasy of the "Other" as the fearful barbarian at the gate or the exotic geisha, that fantasy has helped to sustain the "West"'s own illusions of itself as a rational, masculine, and powerful being.

It is difficult to remember and articulate my experiences as a gay Asian. Things that were so shocking and so clear when I came out, are now chalky and blurry. I remember one guy coming up to me and saying "I love Vietnamese boys." I should have told him that we cooked our rice in Oil of Olay and walked away. Instead, I smiled dumbly and nodded.

The frightening thing is incidents like this no longer shock because I've grown so used to them. They are part of my "common sense" view of reality. But in order to effect change, I must understand where I came from and where I want to go.

But first, a few road signs. Firstly, when I talk about Asian men, I am referring specifically to East Asian gay men — the "yellow" experience as writer and video-maker Richard Fung likens it, as opposed to the "brown" experience of South Asians. I think even though East Asian men are racially oppressed, our experiences of racism are, on the whole, different from our South Asian brothers.

Secondly, when I say gay, I mean gay men. I don't discuss the issue of gender which is an important omission considering that we are Asian men with male privilege. Asian women are consumed differently than Asian men by the North American culture and it is necessary to make links across male gender privilege. However, as an exploration into gay Asian culture and politics, I need to first establish the ground I stand on before making any overtures to dialogue.

Thirdly, by focusing primarily on Asian/white relations, it's inevitable that I will reinforce the powerful position the white gay male already occupies as the "norm" against which I and other gays of colour define our sexuality. I will attempt to avoid some of that by unpacking the term Asian to show how race is first and foremost a complex fiction that directs how power is maintained and distributed, rather than a natural fact.

Part of the title "Explorations...," meanwhile, reflects the provisional status of this book. Even though it will inevitably be seen as representative in the vacuum of Asian gay representation, it is in no way meant to represent the breadth of Asian gay culture.

Some people may be also curious to know why we've included a piece by white gay writer Tim McCaskell entitled "Towards a Sexual Economy of Rice Queenliness" in a book about Asian gay culture.

This is an editorial decision I arrived at with my friends. We want to hear what white guys have to say rather than have us put words in their mouths. In this sense, I wish there were more pieces by non-Asian writers reflecting on their position in Asian gay culture today.

For gay Asians, coming out into a gay community dominated by white Anglo culture is both a liberating and painful experience. The gay community provides a space where we can affirm our sexuality. But, as Fung puts it, "it is at the same time a site of pain and humiliation" where the contradictions of being gay and Asian are exposed.

In his landmark essay "Looking For My Penis: The Eroticized Asian in Gay Video Porn," Fung notes how Asian men in North America are desexualized even while we are socialized into European standards of beauty. Thus, "if Asian men have no sexuality, how can we have homosexuality?" he asks.[1]

The pain of being a gay Asian, however, is not just the pain of direct discrimination but the pain of being negated again and again by a culture that doesn't acknowledge my presence. I remember when I came out, I didn't even know I was "Asian." I thought I was like everyone else — just gay. But of course, I wasn't treated like my white friends. While they were out on dates or partying, I was home reading books, getting quietly politicized.

I had identified so completely with my oppressor that it took me two years to attach the word "racism" to my experiences. It took years longer to fully realize my unique issues as an Asian fag. Not only did I need to come out as a gay man, I also needed to come out as an "Asian". Not only did I have to deal with the question of sexual invisibility as a gay man, there was also the issue of racial invisibility.

In Ottawa with its straight narrow streets, colonial buildings with green copper roofs, and a population that was as white as its long, bitter winters, I searched for images of myself. Although there were plenty of images of men, they were all of white men. The longer I searched, the more disenchanted I became with the gay community that claimed to include or represent me. I remember going out to gays bars and feeling like I was drowning — the whiteness was so complete.

Even in larger cities like Toronto, things were not much better. Despite more coloured faces, it still seemed like the only places I saw myself reflected were in the bars or in the back of gay newspapers and magazines in the classified. I was, by the looks of it, a member of an "exotic" species, infrequently sighted and rarely understood.

Therefore, it is no wonder that a clear and constant theme in many of the stories in this book is the question "How Do I Look?" When we look in the mirror and see a stereotype, who do we believe, the mirror or ourselves?

It is a theme in both Wayne Yung's short story "Brad: December 19, 1992" and Kirby

Hsu's "GOM." As a search for racial and sexual identity that, initially at least, leads them both into the arms of a rice queen, it is a familiar theme in many gay Asians' lives.

Alienated from our own sexuality, the only way we became sexualized is through the predatory consumption of a rice queen. With little presence in the Western erotic imagination, we find we have even less power when it comes to our presence on the sexual menu, except as "boy toys" for white men.

I remember one bar in Toronto called "Chaps" where a lot of gay Asians used to congregate. It had a section called "China Bridge" because that's where a lot of Asians hung out. It was also a hunting ground for rice queens.

While white men cruised looking for their prey, most Asians stood back, lined up against the wall like beauty pageant queens waiting to be chosen. I know because I was one of them. With all the attention focused on white guys, I instinctively knew that as a gay Asian, I rarely had the power to choose and would always be the one chosen.

Looking back, it's amazing how few of us were able to turn to each other for love and support. If we didn't view each other as competitors vying for the love of the white man, we saw each other as "sisters" for whom the thought of sex would have been incestuous. Rarely were we able to see the romantic potential in each other even if we saw it in white men old enough to be our fathers and grandfathers:

> *Q.* What do you call an Asian who likes White guys?
> A. Potato queen.
> *Q.* What do you call a White guy who likes Asians?
> A. Rice queen.
> *Q.* What do you call a White guy who likes other White guys?
> A. Normal.[2]

According to the dominant culture, I could never date another Asian and be normal — I had to be one or the other.

The three pieces by Justin Chin carry on the critique of a white gay monoculture that codes race and racism in terms of a hierarchy of looks and desirability. If, as Fung writes, white men and white male beauty are still the norm against which we judge ourselves and our brothers, where does the "orientalised" Asian male fit in?[3] With his "shiny black hair," "smooth body" and the "forever-12" look? Obviously only in "orientalist" fantasies, as a spicy side-dish in the vast buffet of white bodies that is served daily in bars and baths.

Creating a Radical Asian Gay Culture

If "Queer 'n Asian" has been readily taken up as a slogan for Asian gay empowerment, Kirby Hsu in "GOM" critiques the notion of an Asian gay identity that consumes all other identities.

The continent of "Asia" stretches from the Pacific to the Indian ocean and hosts hundreds of different cultures, religions and languages. So what does it mean for someone to claim that they're "Asian" as if they can just be one thing? Meanwhile, what is gay sex but another name for an infinite number of bodily pleasures?

As Fung explains: "Asian consciousness only begins to eclipse the national conscious-

4

ness in the context of white racism and particularly as experienced in the diaspora."[4] "It is premised on a shared sense of visibility, and less on any common cultural, aesthetic, or religious roots."[5]

In this sense, "Asian" and "gay" are not "natural" differences, but differences that have been highlighted and hierarchically ordered. These "differences" are created precisely in order to be exploited. Racism doesn't exist because there are different races. The "difference" of race exists because there is racism.

To internalize "Asian" as my identity is therefore to see myself as an outsider would see me, where the rich cultural and historical specificity of my Korean culture is homogenized and erased, while permitting the oppressor to dwell in his cultural ignorance.

So how do I reject a term that has been given to me by the dominant Eurocentric culture to represent and control me and, in its place, create new names for my experiences? The language makes it impossible for me as a gay Asian to ask for equality in the gay community and still retain my unique identity as an Asian. The language makes me choose between being equal or different, between racism or homophobia as the lesser of two evils.

Fucking with the White Monoculture

I always consider the difficulty of representing myself in an imperialist language of English which is also my second language. As a repository of traditions and experiences not my own, how do I write in English even as it threatens to unwrite me? How can I express myself in a language that has no words for the reality of my existence? This difficulty is a major focus of Chen Lin's work.

While silence often seems to be the only alternative, naming our experiences is the first step to creating an Asian gay culture that honours both our differences and similarities to whites in the gay community. As both of Lin's short stories and Chi-Wai Au's vignettes show, as Asian gays, our family ties and obligations often compete directly against the individualized existence of being gay in North America.

Creating an Asian gay culture may be the only way to overcome what Richard Fung describes as the "cultural schizophrenia" of Asian gay existence in which "I related on the one hand to a heterosexual family that affirmed my ethnic culture and, on the other hand, to a gay community that was predominantly white."[6]

The task of the Asian gay artist is to both critique and to resignify the terms of our oppression to create complex images of Asian gay men beyond stereotypes of the dominant gay culture. This is part of creating a culture of resistance.

Artist Ho Tam highlights and manipulates exotic stereotypes of Asian men to ground his own identity. His paintings are about exorcising the twin ghosts of invisibility and exoticism while forging new Asian gay identities.

If Tam uses his Chinese background as a focus for his identity, Nguyen Tan Hoang and Vincente Golveo attempt to create the possibility of Asian male desirability. They place the Asian male body within a visual field of consumption usually occupied by "Calvin Klein's pretty white girls and boys." They use these images to unsettle viewer's expectations of encountering white models of beauty. This is what subverts and claims white codes of beauty for Asians. They expose the idea of "beauty" as an expression of society's prejudices and a tool of ideology.

Their image *Camp* is particularly effective for exposing the increasingly consumer-oriented gay culture. The packaging of gay lives by advertisers and gay "lifestyle" magazines represents a trend in gay consumerism where bodily stimulation becomes a model for human relations. By naming the places where US war atrocities were committed as "camp" or gay culture, they re-situate the North American gay movement in the global context, thus exposing its growing ethnocentrism and irrelevance.

The final two stories by Hsu are both a personal testimonial about living with AIDS and a retelling of the "Fairytale of Ms Saigon." As a retelling where the Asian guy ends up leaving the "evil" white man for another Asian, while the white guy commits suicide, it belongs on the bookshelves among other joyously politically-correct bedtime stories of the '90s.

Taking inspiration from classical Greek mythology, the drawings by the artist Nhan Duc Nguyen show how Asian gays can raid white culture and create our own unique hybrid culture. Culture is never stagnant nor produced in isolation. Understanding this is both an opportunity and a challenge. The opportunity is that we can create our culture just by living and by expressing ourselves.

The challenge is producing and circulating our culture. This is a dangerous act that requires the support of people who share in our struggles. Even if that is often a small community of one or two, I am eternally grateful to the help and advice of my "lotus sister" Wayne Yung, publisher Regan McClure, designer Kevin Louis who did a yeoman's job, and tai-tai (great-auntie) Richard Fung who provided the inspiration and insight for much of this work.

* * * * *

Notes:

1. Richard Fung, "Looking for My Penis: The Eroticized Asian in Gay Video Porn," *How Do I Look: Queer Film and Video*, edited by Bad Object-Choices, (Seattle, Bay Press: 1991), pg 148.
2. Wayne Yung, *Beyond Yellow Fever*, chapbook, (Vancouver, Pomelo Projects: 1995).
3. Fung, "Looking for My Penis," pg 149.
4. Fung, "Looking Yellow, Asian Identities in Film and Video," *The State of Asian America: Activism and Resistance in the 1990s*, edited and introduced by Karin Aguilar-San Juan, (Boston, South End Press: 1994), pg 162.
5. Fung, "Looking Yellow," pg 162.
6. Fung, "Looking for My Penis," pg 149.

ARTIST STATEMENT

Wayne Yung

"Brad: December 22, 1992" is a snapshot from my pilgrimage in search of my sexual and racial identity. As a gay Canadian, I lust for the snow-skinned Adonis; yet as a gay Chinese, I stand outside the forbidden city of "gay white male seeks same." If beauty and love are the white man, can I be beautiful and beloved? Growing up gay and Asian in Edmonton, it has been a struggle to discover the romantic potential in myself and my brothers.

For a gay male alone among straights, it can be difficult to imagine the romantic potential of same-gender love. Gay writing is often the spark that inflames the romantic imagination. Homoerotic fiction is rich with fantasy lovers, from English aristocrats to Midwestern farmboys to Fire Island disco queens. The promise of cruising blue eyes and sweaty blond hair beckons. In a world of love liberated, there is a place for each of us.

Unless, of course, you're not a sweaty, blue-eyed blond. There is no place for Asian men in the romantic imaginations of most Canadians, straight or gay. There is no Chinese lover in the rose garden, the hayloft, the tea dance. He belongs in the laundry, not the bar; in the restaurant, not the bedroom.

His one apparent refuge is in the arms of a rice queen. Then, the stone-faced eunuch becomes a dark-smiling geisha, arms swaying to the flute and drum. After standing outside the bedroom door, the dancing feels good. Eventually, however, the kimono becomes a straitjacket. The burden of exotic stereotyping can be just as painful as sexual invisibility.

My writing today explores the struggle to establish a gay Asian identity that is somewhere between the the emasculate and the exotic. It shifts the focus from "gay white male seeks same" to "gay Asian male seeks other." As gay writers honour the unique beauty of men loving men, I honour the distinct beauty of the Asian lover.

In the end, queer writing is not about any sexual preference in particular, but about the diversity of preference. It is the affirmation and celebration of the varieties of love. Asian sexuality is a vital part of the larger sexual community, and love and sex are alive and well among those of the 'Asian persuasion.'

"Brad: December 19, 1992"*

WAYNE YUNG

Grazing through electric blue fields of late-night television, Jack's eyes glowed neon. Soft, milky flesh sagged into the beige velour of the recliner. In the cool aurora, his briefs glowed like polar ice, and fine blond hair sparked like static on his skin. His palm cradled a sleek remote control, the thumb pulsing against the buttons with a movement as subtle as the dreaming eye.

The phone purred, like a kitten. Absently, his fingers rooted under an inky nest of newspapers.

"Hello?"

"Hi. Is this Jack?"

"Yeah." His eyes remained locked on the far blue horizon.

"This is Brad Wong, from Calgary. I replied to your ad."

"Uh-huh."

"I've just arrived at the bus depot." There was a hiss of static. "In the ad you said I could stay the night. I was wondering— is the offer still open?"

With a blink, his vision snapped back from the distance. "Sure," he said. They arranged to meet in twenty minutes, at a nearby hotel lobby.

He turned off the television and drifted through the velvet darkness of the hallway. Like a sleepwalker, he tracked his footprints by memory.

The bedroom was dim with starlight. His fingers traced the carved relief of the wardrobe and skimmed across the mirror, seeking the door seam. The double doors opened with a gentle push. By touch, he chose a pair of faded jeans, hollowed to the contours of his flesh. Over his pale, icy skin, he pulled a dark cableknit sweater, bearded and torn with age.

Pale blue digital numbers floated in the dim recesses of the top shelf of the wardrobe. Reaching overhead, his fingers scanned the braille of machine buttons. He pressed one, and a tiny pair of eyes flared in the shadows above, one red, one green. Satisfied, he closed the doors.

The hotel lobby was worn red carpets and polished wood. Brad sat in a tapestried armchair, his face suffused with the glow from a yellow silk lampshade. A warm pool of light spread beneath the lamp's fringes and fell on the plaid carpetbag that slouched by his knee.

"Hi," said Jack, offering a handshake. Brad's long, fine fingers were wet and cold, but the grip was surprisingly strong. "Have you waited long?"

"No."

"Good." Jack hefted the bag and slung it over his shoulder. "Then let's go."

He led Brad through the cold tunnel of streetlight, overarched by naked iron trees and concrete towers. Snow fell, lightly. Quietly, they spoke of minor things, and soon were at the apartment.

"Can I make you some coffee?"

"Tea."

Jack filled a copper kettle and set it on the stove. The boy crossed the sand-coloured linoleum to warm his fingers by the burner. Stepping behind him, Jack began massaging his shoulders and felt them sag with relief. "So tense," he said.

"Long bus ride. Sixteen hours."

*Originally published in Queeries: Anthology of Gay Male Prose.

His hands circled around Brad's chest, drawing him close. "How old are you?"

"Twenty-one."

"You look much younger."

Brad shrugged. Jack rested his chin on the shoulder, as they kept vigil over the steady blue flames under the kettle.

"You must be tired. Why don't we sit in the living room?" He led Brad to the floral beige chesterfield. They sank into its padded cushions, sliding on the sleek velour. Casually, Jack draped one arm around Brad's shoulders, and stretched his legs onto the glass-topped coffee table.

Brad's eyes studied the room, avoiding Jack's steady gaze. After a moment, the man gently kissed his neck. He shrugged with surprise, and pushed Jack away.

"You don't waste any time, do you?"

"I'm overcome by your beauty."

Brad smiled, unbelieving. The kettle whistled, and Jack rose.

When he returned with the tea, he found Brad by the tall pine bookcases, head cocked, reading the titles.

"You like to travel?"

"Yes," replied Jack.

"You've been to all these places?" Fingers fanned the titles.

"No. But I like to read about them." He poured the tea. "How do you take it?"

"Black." He accepted the bone china cup. It clattered slightly on the saucer, then was still.

"You travel much?"

"No," replied Brad. "But I want to." He turned away, and sipped his tea. "I like it here, in Vancouver. There are men, like you... who like Chinese."

"But not in Calgary?"

"No. They like cowboys with moustaches and big muscles." With a wry smile, he produced the small hard lump of his bicep. Impulsively, Jack bent to kiss it. He laid his hands on Brad's waist, and then sank his lips into the boy's neck.

Abruptly, Brad pulled back. "Not so fast, okay?"

Jack shrugged. He turned and gestured at the television. "Do you want to watch some movies?"

"What do you have?"

"I've got some porn: some straight, some gay."

Brad was silent. "Do you have any with Asians?"

"Just one. From Thailand. It's kinda boring, though."

He considered. "I want to see it."

Jack turned on the television, and turned off the lamp. The movie opened in a men's shower. One young man knelt before another, water dripping down his brown chest. Their were no voices, just 60's rock guitar.

"I've never seen Orientals have sex before."

"It's hard to find."

"Does this one have any white guys?"

"No."

After a few minutes, Brad picked up the remote and the sex abruptly sped by. The quiet darkness was warmed by the hum of the spinning motor.

"What is it you like about Chinese guys?"

Jack thought for a moment. "The skin," he said. "It's so smooth and golden. And I like black hair, and brown eyes." He ran his fingers through Brad's hair.

"I'm not attracted to Oriental men."

"No? Why not?"

"I don't know. I've only been with white men."

The video shifted to three young men in a daisy chain.

"Do you sleep with white men too?" Brad asked.

"Not often." He reached over and took a sip from Brad's teacup. "I don't like them. Too heavy, and crude, especially in the face. I sleep with them only if they're young and thin and absolutely hairless." He stroked Brad's cheek. "Even then, I don't like pale skin, blond hair, blue eyes."

Brad turned to face him. "Even yourself? You're blond, blue-eyed."

"Me?" He considered this for a moment, as the boys on screen sped to orgasm. "I've never really thought about it before. Men have always been attracted to me." He turned to Brad with a sly grin. "Especially Asians. They like blonds."

Brad smiled. "But you don't."

Jack twisted the black hair with his fingers. "I don't mind being blond. But I like sleeping with men who have black hair. Maybe it's like salt and pepper shakers." He kissed the boy on the cheek, gently. "I'm happy with who I am. I just happen to prefer making love with Orientals. And, hopefully, they like to make love with me."

Brad lowered his eyes and smiled before turning back to the television. Two boys were necking in the back room of a grocery store.

"When I was a kid, I always wanted to be white."

Jack kissed his ear. "I'm glad you're not." He nuzzled his nose into the soft neck, breathing in the moist heat. "I like the way you smell. Like Chinese food."

Brad laughed. "You'll be hungry again in an hour."

"I hope so."

Abruptly, the video cut to snow.

Jack stood, and turned off the TV. In the darkness, Brad saw Jack's silent black silhouette stretch and yawn against the deep indigo sky.

"How about a massage?" asked the man quietly.

"Okay."

He offered his hand and led Brad down the darkened hallway.

The wide bed was wrinkled with white cotton sheets. As they undressed, Jack admired the graceful arc of Brad's figure. The boy stretched out across the bed on his stomach, and Jack crouched naked astride the boy's thighs. His warm, dry hands kneaded Brad's shoulders firmly. His strokes were deep, slow, and deliberate. Gently, he traced the length of the spine with his fingertips, each pass punctuated with a warm, dry kiss, one below the other, in a path that led to the crack.

Jack inched his body onto the calves. Stretching like a cat, he milked the buns, then spread them, and nuzzled his nose and tongue deep into the groove. Brad moaned. His hips bucked as his spine arched. The pelvis ground slowly into Jack's face. He reached under and gripped the hard, stiff snake that lay there.

He crawled up Brad's body, and embraced him. His lips sought a kiss, but the boy turned his face and offered his neck. Jack's sandpaper cheeks rasped against the tender flesh.

His kisses drifted down the boy's body as the torso squirmed and writhed like a snared eel. Jack took the cock in his mouth, but Brad withdrew. His hands pulled at the man's scalp, mashing his cheeks into the inner thighs.

Jack nudged the boy's head down to his own crotch, but the mouth would not cross the edge of his bush. The lips dragged across his belly, with no trace of tongue. Finally, Jack took the slender fingers and wrapped them around his cock. Cupping the boy's hand with his own, he brought his fever to peak, and relief.

The boy lay still under the weight of the other man's semen. After a moment, Jack moved to take the boy's rocky erection into his own mouth.

"No." Brad gripped Jack's hair, restraining him like a cat by its tail. "Not tonight."

Jack looked into the boy's hooded almond eyes, shadowed by the moonlight, and could read nothing there. He shrugged.

They showered together, Jack's lathered hands slithering down the smooth yellow body. Brad finished first, and Jack followed a few minutes later. When he returned to the bedroom, the boy was already asleep. He slid under the sheets and spooned Brad from behind, wrapping his arm around so that his palm lay over the sleeping heart.

The next night, they went to a nightclub. Amidst the thunderous glamour and steaming smoke, Brad was silent, watchful as a child at the edge of a playground. Friends came to greet Jack but faded away as Jack's mute shadow became apparent. He made no mention of Brad, no introductions. They barely acknowledged each other's presence but, even without contact, their connection was palpable, an invisible string that connected hand to hand, foot to foot.

Without a word, Brad pulled Jack into the sweaty crush of hard bodies. He raised his arms and they swayed overhead like golden cobras while his narrow waist writhed and twisted under the circle of Jack's grip. A musky sweat rose from the boy's flesh. Jack felt the distant eyes watching, dark with smoky envy. Lost in dance, dreaming, the boy was blind to cruising glances.

That night, their sex was harder, stronger, driven by a rhythm deeper and more urgent than their beating hearts. Jack stared into the hooded depths of Brad's eyes with a silent appeal. With a nod, the boy assented. As he watched the latex being rolled down the man's shaft, his fingers stroked the thighs, idly, as if waiting for the bass beat to resume.

The thrusts began slow and deep, and the boy sounded each new depth with a moan. Jack's rhythm became more and more jerky until, with a silent shout, his body exploded and collapsed. His sphincter clenched with every pulse of the boy's heart and Jack twitched with the memory of agony. After an eternal silence, he kissed Brad's neck, and cheek, and lips.

"I love you," he said.

Brad smiled and pulled Jack's torso down onto his own so that his face was hidden.

Hours later he woke to find Jack slouched against a pillow, with a cigarette in his fingers, and a can of beer on his belly. A television sat in the corner like Buddha, alive but silent. Brad's shoulder nestled into Jack's armpit, his cheek against the heart. It was enough to touch, and to hear the hidden drum that pulsed under the thin layer of moist heat.

Brad's attention shifted to the tall, dark wardrobe that faced the foot of the bed. The doors were ornate with carved relief. Two large mirrors, half-circles, were set in the centre. The liquid glass surface reflected snowy peaks of cotton sheets from which rose two breathing mountains, the raven-peaked one leaning against the fair.

"It's bad luck to put a mirror in front of a marriage bed," said Brad.

"Who says?"

"My grandmother. She says that love is reversed in the mirror, and comes back as hate."

Jack took a long drag on his cigarette and held it. As he spoke again, his words appeared smoke-coloured.

"Do you love me?"

Brad paused. "No."

"Good. Then there's nothing to worry about."

The next evening, Brad returned at dusk. Jack welcomed him with a kiss and led him to the candlelit dining room. Two solemn flames were matched by their reflections, suspended in the mellow depths of the lacquered mahogany table.

They shared a salad of butter lettuce and nasturtium, with a slender bottle of golden herbal wine. Jack fed asparagus to Brad with his fingers before unwrapping the salmon baked in foil. Afterwards, there was a pot of chrysanthemum tea with white petals floating on the amber liquid.

That evening, they made love quietly and tenderly. They spoke little and, afterwards, Brad showered alone. When they parted, he didn't offer his phone number, and Jack didn't ask. His bus left at midnight.

Weeks later, Jack was at home, alone. In the bedroom, he undressed slowly and deliberately by the cool light of the streetlight below and the starlight above. From the wardrobe, he took a new pair of briefs, crisp and white inside the crackling cellophane. He tore the package open and breathed in its clean fragrance, smothering his muzzle in the crisp cotton. He slid it up over his ankles, dragging it over his thighs to finally stretch and cling to his pelvis.

Overhead, in the darkness of the top shelf, his fingertips skimmed across the spines of video tapes. Groping blindly, his fingers found the last tape and retrieved it. On the matte plastic was a stark white label: "BRAD: DECEMBER 19, 1992."

As if sleepwalking, he drifted through the darkened hallway to the living room. With a touch of his fingertip, the video machine awoke, and the television screen ignited with a crackle of static. The padded velour recliner sagged as it received the weight of his milky flesh. As the video played, Jack's eyes focused on the far horizon far beyond the ghostly image of two bodies making love in a starlit field of white cotton sheets.

Somewhere, under a light cover of newspaper, the phone softly purred.

ARTIST STATEMENT

Kirby Hsu

Born in Hong Kong, I came to Canada at the age of 14 with my family. A consciousness of being a gay Asian developed much later in my twenties during my seven year relationship with a Jamaican-Chinese and a gradual involvement with Gay Asians of Toronto. My process of self-discovery and struggle for acceptance continues to date in the face of AIDS. Feeling ignored and marginalized by the mainstream, gay, and Asian communities, I started to explore issues of culture and gay Asian identity through different media.

GOM (Script from Video, 9 minutes, 1994)

KIRBY HSU

In my dream I was searching again. The sky was clear and sunny. The breeze was warm. I wanted to get somewhere. A hotel, a beach, a shop, maybe a home. I knew exactly where I wanted to go and how to get there. But the streetcar didn't come, the elevator didn't stop, corridors only went into endless corridors. I kept moving with all my strength in the direction I had to go. It was, however, always just beyond my reach.

My searching sometimes takes me to my birth place. I was born in Hong Kong, the pearl of the Orient. I guess that makes me an Oriental. Or is a pearl of the Orient like an Oriental pearl? I actually have an aunt named Pearl. It was a popular name from that era, so was Ruby, Suzie, and Jade. But my parents wouldn't let me call myself Pearl. It's too rich for you, they would say. So I had to compromise, I humbly called myself Lotus Blossom.

Even though I have the slant eyes and the flat nose, I discovered recently that I'm not really Chinese. My friends from China set me straight on that one. A Chinese, you see, is from China, that means the Republic of China. Me, *moi,* on the other hand, was born as a British subject in the crown colony of Hong Kong. A subject of Great Britain without official status.

To avoid arguments, nowadays, I prefer to call myself Asian. This might have solved some of my problems but not some other ones. The gay Asian organization in my city will not permit white guys to participate in decision making because they are not Asian. It is a matter of self-empowerment, really. A white guy regardless of whether he was born in Asia will not be accepted as an Asian, whereas an Asian born in North America, who is completely American acculturated, will be considered Asian without question. Some of my ABC, American Born Chinese, friends are less Asian in cultural mentality than some of my white friends. Once again, I'm searching. I don't know if being an Asian is defined by place of birth, cultural identification, or by skin colour.

It was so long ago. I can't even remember when it was that I found out my sexual attraction to men is called being gay. I was brought up in a fairly liberal family, some might call it Westernized. I didn't have a problem with my homosexual preference. It never crossed my mind that it was a sin, a sickness, or an abnormality. But somehow from deep within my consciousness, I knew I was different from other people and I was supposed to keep quiet about it.

The Chinese culture is very rigid in some ways but it can also be very accommodating in other ways. Yes, the white guys love our versatility. I figured out with my friends the other day that there is an acceptable way of being gay in the Chinese culture, and that is if you first fulfill your familial obligations. I respect my elders and take care of them. I went through university and completed my education. Now, I have a good secure job. Even though I've failed to get married and contribute to the family lineage, my older brother has already done that. By virtue of my success and respect for them, my family lets me be gay. We just don't talk about it.

* * * * *

Shortly after coming out, I discovered that being gay and desirable means you have to be white, young, blond, and muscular. Somehow all of them also seem to have big cocks with balls of bulls. Being a blank slate to gay culture, the only people I thought worthy of going after were the clone types. The common American folk diet of meat, potato and buns. I have to confess to you that, yes, yes, yes, I was a potato queen.

One time in my early days, I had sex with this gorgeous white guy in a bathhouse. He seemed to have left my room in an awful hurry afterwards so I went looking for him. When I finally found him and inquired as to where he was, he said, obviously where you were not. I learned quickly that there are guys who would have sex with you, would let you suck their cocks and fuck them up the ass, but would not acknowledge you at other times. They merely target Asians for sex. I discovered rice-queens. The first time was devastating but then, first times are usually devastating. Eventually, I learned to sympathize with my local gay Asian association.

To be honest, I was basically a skinny Chinese geek, an average nerd, generally ignored by the larger gay community. It's no fun when you want to be disco queen and you end up being a wall flower queen. So I figured I had to do something to make myself more attractive. Well, I thought at least I could try adding more muscle to my body. Working out once a week at first didn't seem enough to make up for my years of impoverishment. So I started going to the gym two times a week. That didn't do anything either. Ok, ok, I encouraged myself to persevere. I started going three times a week. Then I was ready to move into the gym altogether. I almost gave up my apartment. Maybe my father was right after all — developing your muscle precludes development of your intellect. I was merely doing a "Revenge of the Nerds" number. That was my muscle queen phase.

My fixation with white guys got turned upside down when I met this Asian. He was of Chinese origin but born in Jamaica and very, very cute. He looked Asian but didn't speak a word of Chinese. Culturally, he went to school and was educated in the U.S. For the first time, I was able to find beauty in an Asian because I was not turned off by his "Asian-ness." A whole new world was opened up to me. I started to turn into sticky rice. I've had sex with many white guys in my lifetime and I've had three relationships. All my relationships were with Asians. In fact, many of my Asian friends complain that they can't settle down because they have such good sex with white guys but get along so much better with Asians. Yes, you white guys can flatter yourselves, you are just as exotic to us as we are to you. By the way, this is sticky rice you're looking at.

Recently, one of my dear white friends with a self-proclaimed incurable obsession for Asians asked me why it was that he has had a number of experiences with Asian guys who would call him up and they would go out to dinner, go on trips, go to concerts, go to movies, but side-track him whenever it was time to go to bed. It's not that they were closeted or anything, and the rice-queen was not a UFO — ugly, fat or old. Actually, he had been butterflied. I told him to study characters in *M. Butterfly* a play by David Henry Hwang. Do not go see the movie, by the way. Even though my white friends thought John Lone was lovely playing a woman in that movie, all my Asian friends unanimously agreed that John Lone looked more like a drag queen or else the ugliest Chinese woman we know.

Rice, potato, and other perversities. We don't need stereotypes. We are all unique. Don't we know that? But do gay Asians have anything in common? Is rice really different from potato? If you ask me, the only thing I would think of doing with potato nowadays is to make French fries.

Nhan Duc Nguyen

Nhan Duc Nguyen is a Vancouver artist. His recent exhibitions include Temple of My Familiar *in Belfast, Ireland, and* Cocksure: At Times I... *in Vancouver.*

ARTIST STATEMENT

Ho Tam

Ho Tam is an artist living in Toronto. His work has been exhibited in cities across North America, including YYZ Artists' Outlet (Toronto), A Space (Toronto), Galerie SAW Video (Ottawa), AKA Artists' Centre (Saskatoon), Artspeak (Vancouver), Observatorie 4 (Montreal), and White Columns (New York).

The term "Big Circle Boys" is taken from the name of an Asian criminal gang in China. Tam deliberately chose it for its controversy and ambiguity, its references to certain sexual practices, as well as to the "symbolic mapping of a sub-culture within the larger picture of our society."

"Big Circle Boys" is composed of three groups of work:

Self Portraits/Icons addresses the relationship between self image and representation in society. Large canvases of "godly and gaudy" gold paint set the background for haloed male nudes on the labels of Asian food products.

Matinee Idols (not shown here) juxtaposes portraits of young Asian actors and labels with names from advertising and the mass media.

Greetings combines logos of common household products with images of male genitalia.

Throughout these works, Tam combines fragmented and detached visual memories, seeking to broaden perspectives and possibilities for the interpretation and reinvention of his own self image.*

*from YYZ gallery press release

97-Chink, or Baby, How Do I Look Tonight?

JUSTIN CHIN

I
How Do I Look?

Rule #1: Everyone is White unless stated otherwise.

Example: Joe, Sam, an African-American, and their Asian-American friend Stanley went on a picnic at the beach where they met Thereza, a Latina, and her friend Jane.

Hence,
Sample Question #1: Who is White?
Model Answer #1: Joe and Jane.

Sample Question #2: If the five characters are arrested at the beach for indecent exposure, whose ethnicity will be named in the local newspaper?
Model Answer #2: Sam, Stanley and Thereza.

Sample Question #3: If a news photographer shows up and takes pictures of the picnic, who will be prominently featured in the gay news weekly and who will be the only one named in the caption?
Model Answer #3: Joe.

* * * * *

Like all male bodies in gay culture, everything is predicated on the image and concepts of the beautiful body. If the average gay man is to stroll through the racks of titillating images, he will see a vast buffet of White bodies, and at the end of the buffet table are the "splashes of colour that make any buffet table entertaining."

The gay Asian male body, however, is a different creature and certain rules apply to it. For the uninitiated, who are eager to learn and experience more, here are some things that you must know about the gay Asian body that will help you in your research as you peruse the racks at your local bookstore or library:

1. The desired image is buffed & muscular or slim & lean.
2. Body hair and/or fat is utterly undesirable.
3. Severe ectomorphism becomes a fetishistic quality.
4. Nipples are not important and are never emphasized.
5. The background and the objects surrounding the body are almost as important as the body.

Suggested backgrounds and objects are: i) Oriental vases and urns; ii) Masks and costumes representing ancient dynastic histories; iii) Silk; iv) Bamboo, pussy willows and the most potent object of all, chrysanthemums.

(True testimony/verbatim transcript:)

"Hello. My name is Peter Wong. And (squeak). Hello? Hello? Yes. My name is Peter Wong and I am a real person, not a paid model. Like most Chinese men, I used to be very frigid and uptight in bed but ever since I started surrounding my pillows with chrysanthemums...

"Ever since I've surrounded my bed with chrysanthemums, man, I've been fucking and sucking like the horniest cow this side of the Yang Ho River. My repertoire of sex acts has expanded and the other day, I used this bottle of mazola corn oil, 6 pounds of cooked spam and..."

* * * * *

Primary Sources

The Nob Hill Cinema's Asian Week runs an advertisement in the local gay newsweekly. Year after year, the strip joint features a week of Asian male performers. Year after year, they do not use a real photograph to advertise the week, only drawings of buffed Asian men with headbands inscribed with some Oriental language. (For headbands, see *The Karate Kid* Parts 1 through 3.) When a real photo was finally used, it was of the group of Asian male dragon boat racers ripped out from a travel catalogue. The photo reduced to a small strip hides behind Chip Daniels' and Senior Latino's hips, the other main attraction.

The promotional image that most sticks to my mind is one from two years ago. Asian Week was featured with a drawing of a buffed Japanese man in a headband and a jock-strap, tied in Oriental rope harness fashion. He is gagged. His legs are bound and his hands are tied behind his back. His eyes are simultaneously vacant and intense. There is a tube of lube beside him and a huge black dildo lying on the floor, pointing at his perineum.

Sample Question #1: Who is using the dildo on the cartoon Japanese man?
Sample Question #2: Does the cartoon Japanese man enjoy it?
Sample Question #3: Can the cartoon Japanese man protest if he doesn't enjoy it?
Sample Question #4: Will the cartoon Japanese man protest if he doesn't enjoy it?
Sample Question #5: Is this just a cartoon?

II
How Do I Sound?

Hello.
This is 97-CHINK.
If you want to play, you must press your Visa or Mastercard number. Now.
If you want a submissive Oriental houseboy to do your laundry then suck your dick, press 1. Now.
If you want a Thai go-go boy to touch his body on stage just for you, press 2. Now.
If you want a hot hung Filipino youth to worship your body, press 3. Now.
If you like an alternative menu, press 4.
For voice mail, press 5. Now.

(xxx-xxx-xxxx-xxxx). #. beep. 2. #.

Hello. My name is Huang. I just come in from working in the paddy field and boy, I tell you, am I sweaty, I must take a bath. I like taking showers because it makes me feel so clean. Here, I leave the door open so you can talk to me while I shower, okay. Ooh. The water feels so good on my skin. I got very good skin, very soft even though I work in the sun and get real good tan. Do you like to feel my skin? That's okay, I don't mind you feeling my skin. It's so soft, yah? Oh, I'm so silly, I forgot to bring the soap with me. Can you please get it for me? Thank you, you are so kind. Oh. I can't reach my back. Please, can you please help me? Ooh yes, you are too kind. I must get super clean, please scrub harder. Oh yes. Thank you. Please, don't soap close to my private parts otherwise I get hard and then I get very shy. Oh dear, my cock is now getting hard from all that soap water. Oh no, if I go out now, my father will see my cock standing and he will get angry, what should I do. What? Okay, but please, gently okay? I'm very scared doing this. If you use your mouth, it will be gentler than your hand? Okay. But please be careful. I don't ever do this before...

(beep) (#)

Hello. My name is Aurelio Eduardo Conception Batongbacal. But you can call me Eddy because you are my friend. I like watching movies, reading stories, watching TV and making new friends like you. I like to have friends all over the world so I can visit them and they can visit me when they come to Manila and I can show them all the beautiful sights of the city and show them just how beautiful the Philippine culture is. The people are also so friendly. But sometimes I get so lonely because I don't have many gay friends, that's why I'm so happy that you're my friend. I like you because you are so manly. Can I ask you a personal question? Sorry. I shy to ask you. But do you have chest hair? Oh, I like that very much. Can I please feel it? Oh yes, did anyone tell you you look like Magnum? Yes, you do. I think Magnum is very handsome. I think you are very handsome. Is it true that Americans have big, you know. Can I see? Oooo! It's so big. I'm so scared! What? It's not painful? But it's so big. Slowly and easy? Please, you teach me, please? I want to learn how to play with big American cocks, because they are more fun! So you teach Eddy, okay?

(Beep,) Reply: (Hello Lotus Blossom...)

III
Do You Know Me?

Hello. My name is Peter Lum. Do you recognize me? I'm an actor. Perhaps not. Let's try again.

"Hey, do you come to the steam baths often?" Recognize me now? That was the line I used in *Steam Boat Dragons* before I fucked Lance Michaels in the ass.

No? Perhaps you know me by my other name, my stage names: Kimo. Thu Minh. Kwan. Jeong Chew. Chris Fujimoto. Perhaps you know me by my reputation. I'm the only working gay Asian male porn star in America who's a top. You might have seen me in films like *Platoon Dragon, Shanghai Dragons, Dragon Mission, Dragon Meat, Dragons* and *Dragons 2: China Heat.*

Yes. In my first film, *Red Dragon Heat,* the director said for Scott Folberg to fuck me in the ass in a scene at the school gym, but then, Scott was on something and he couldn't get his dick hard so I improvised, and I fucked him in the ass. The scene was hot. And I discovered that I actually can fuck White boys in the ass — and enjoy it too! Wow, what a revelation.

In my last film, *Hard Dragon,* I got to fuck six White boys because I'm the star now. I even get creative input on the shoots and the scene. Like this one scene where I meet Larion Lasley at the doctor's office, I'm supposed to play the janitor while he plays the patient. But I tell the director, "I want to be a doctor!" And so I played a doctor. I don't want to perpetuate stereotypes that Asians are coolies and low-class workers. And in another scene, the director wants me to come in a samurai outfit! But then I tell him, the character is Chinese!!! How can you use a Samurai outfit? So we rewrote the scene. I wore a Kung-Fu outfit instead! These things are important, you know.

But my favourite film is *Penetrate the Dragon.* In this one, I get to fuck this other Asian guy. It was a difficult scene. And I had to prepare myself for days to do it. Later, I found out that the guy I was fucking, Wilson Woo, also had similar fears and had to prepare for days by looking at gay Asian porn magazines and masturbating to them, just like I did. The scene was in the backroom of a Chinese restaurant. He and I are there with our White dates but then we pretend to go to the bathroom while actually we fuck! Great, huh? Then later, our dates discover us and we all fuck! This is a ground breaking porn film for gay Asians, I think.

Anyhow, I don't think I'm going to be in the porn business for long. Too demanding. I mean, I'm lucky that I got a nice big dick that photographs well, but I think I still want to go to college. I want to major in Asian-American Studies and Theatre, you know. One day, I want to make a feature length film about Asian-Americans. In fact, I already have a film script about two hundred pages long with good dialogue, lots of double entendres and symbolism.

IV
But How Do I Really Look?

The Asian Castro Boy: A Study

Kingdom: *Animalia*
Phylum: *Chordate*
Class: *Mammalia*
Order: *Omnivora*
Family: *Hominidae*
Genus: *Homo Sapien*
Species: *Orientali Castronitus*
Habitat: *Castro Street, San Francisco, Unites States of America.*

The *Orientali Castronitus* is primarily found roaming Castro Street between Market Street and 19th Street. Occasionally a few may stray on the smaller side streets. They number in the dozens and are best found all day on Saturday and Sunday, though many are spotted in the evenings too.

Distinguishing Features of Various Species of Orientali Castronitus

1. Orientali Castronitus Fluffinitus

Features: Girbaud. Klein. Ralph Lauren or any outfit bought at trendy overpriced store in not-so-good, but still moderately safe, neighbourhood. Good shoes. Body Glove, spandex, lycra, bicycle shorts (even though they cab everywhere). Tight little denim shorts.

Hair: Well groomed. Moussed—very flammable. Gelled & sculptured into hard shell to protect against elements & worthy to be placed in the middle of a 10-course Chinese dinner. May be hidden under cap on a bad hair day.

Group Site: The Midnight Sun with three pieces of picture ID ready.

Diet: Nouvelle Cuisine. Thai restaurants. Bran Muffin and Diet Coke at Village Deli.

Distinguishing Call: "Discrimination against people of colour? What? I don't know. I'm really not political. I just want to dance and have fun and meet someone cute, okay?"

2. *Orientali Castronitus Withaolius*

Features: Stuck to his White companion. Either on arm, on hip or with invisible leash. Eyes averted to any other White men, but will stare straight into other Asians' eyes, then quickly look away.

Hair: See *Orientali Castronitus Fluffinitus.* Or whatever his companion wants.

Group Site: Wherever his companion wants.

Diet: Thai restaurants, Chinese restaurants, Castro Hibachi (for the ambience and presumably authentic food, the kind that you can eat lots of and still don't gain weight).

Distinguishing Call: "I can't talk to you, my boyfriend is here." "Please don't touch me, I have a boyfriend."

3. *Orientali Castronitus Activistus*

Features: ACT-UP t-shirt or QUEER NATION/UNITED COLORS t-shirt (ripped off sleeves optional). Jeans (rips optional). Necklace thing hanging from neck. Glasses from chic urban designer. Clean polished Doc Martens. In hand or backpack, either i) The collected works of Michel Foucault; ii) The collected poems of Audre Lorde; iii) *Woman, Native, Other* by Trinh T. Minh-Ha; iv) *Queer in America* by Michaelangeo Signorile; or v) *Mandala Symbolism* by C.G. Jung.

Hair: Functional. Bill Clinton-esque. Flat-top.

Group Site: A Different Light. Flyering tables at Castro and 18th. Hot 'n Hunky. Escape from New York Pizza or Marcellos Pizza. Castro Theatre.

Diet: Diner food. 24-hour joint food. Pizza slices.

Distinguishing Call: "Act Up! Fight Back!" "We're Queer! We're Here!" "Die, Gay White Man!" "Asian Power." "Empowerment."

4. *Orientali Castronitus Alternativus*

Features: Black clothes. Bags under eyes. Sneer/growl. Plaid shirts, scruffy Doc Martens or any boots, ripped jeans or cut-off trousers. Knife, tattoos & piercings optional. Alienated aura.

Hair: Buzz cut, shaved, stubble or none.

Group Site: Usually not found in Castro. But may be seen at A Different Light Bookstore or Escape from New York Pizza or sometimes at Castro Theatre.

Diet: Cheap food. Coffee. Alcohol optional.

Distinguishing Call: "Fuck off." "Whaddya want?" "Die Fluffy Scum."

Approaching the *Orientali Castronitus*

While myth and years of conventional wisdom have it that the *Orientali Castronitus* are friendly creatures and may be approached at any time without any repercussions, this has in modern years been proven to be a fallacy.

Some species of the *Orientali Castronitus,* such as the *Fluffinitus* may be approached with ease, the others may not be that easy to approach. For instance, the *Withhaolius* have been known to snap back or run like a startled fawn when approached. In some eyewitness accounts, the *Haole* with the *Withaolius* displayed severely violent territorial behavior. The two most unapproachable are the *Activistus* and the *Alternativus.* The *Activistus* may start yelling at you; and the *Alternativus* may stab you in the gut. Be warned!

Now, that you are familiar with the species *Orientali Castronitus,* feel free to roam the Castro without fear or trepidation of them. If you still wish to learn more about them, you should ask the reference librarian at your local library for books about them , though very little has been written about the subject.

For the adventurous ones who might want to actually approach one of the *Orientali Castronitus,* here are some suggested opening lines:

For the *Fluffinitus:*

1. "Where are you from?"
2. "Where's a good club/restaurant/place to buy shirts around here?"

For the *Withhaolius:*

1. "You're so lucky to have such a good-looking companion."
Note: Always address the companion and not the *Orientali Castronitus.*

For the *Activistus:*

1. "What do you think of (insert name of congressional bill here)?"
2. "I don't understand the issues in this flyer, can you please explain it to me?"

For the *Alternativus:*

1. "How can anyone buy the Sex Pistols on CD, man? That's so stupid! How can you understand its meaning then?"
2. "Who does your tattz, man?'

Note: Though it may seem harmless, NEVER say: "I like your tattoos, what are they actually? Do they mean something?"

V
Do You Love Me?

An Open Letter to Justin Chin
(ACTUAL TRUE LETTER, I no kid you)

My reaction to your awful whining, Justin? Well, I reacted on several different levels. I was immediately struck by the anger, the hatred, the rage, the venom that poured forth from your pen and I thought to myself, "This guy has really been hurt. He's in a lot of pain." And thinking this, my eyes got moist, as indeed they are as I write this. I've never been into S&M. I don't enjoy pain, either my own or someone else's. And when I imagine the pain that you had to go through in order to be filled up with so much rage, my heart goes out to you.

Justin, you seem to rage at everyone: you're angry at us Whites who are prejudiced against Asians; you're angry at those of us who are attracted to Asians and even Asian culture, ridiculing even our mismatched collections of Asian art, our attempts to use chopsticks and to learn other cultural customs. You are even angry at other Asians who are attracted to Whites. I wonder, do you ever wear blue jeans or use a fork?

Justin, none of us likes to be nothing more than a sex object. More than once an Asian has been disappointed in me because I didn't have hair on my chest. And, on the flip side of that, I have experienced many times the silly gushing of an Asian over my blue eyes. But, Justin, in all of these cases, we went beyond that initial reaction and developed relationships (not just sexual ones, either) that were based on more than my blue eyes or their silky smooth hairless skin.

We are all humans, Justin, and how can we explain what it is that makes your crotches tingle? Can you honestly say to us that your own physical attractions to others have been totally without objectification? Have you never experienced fetish-like qualities in your own sexual urges?

Your anger is destroying you, Justin. It is poison that is eating you alive. And that's such a waste. Yes, Justin, there is injustice in this world. There is racism, discord, prejudice, discrimination, evil, pollution, hunger, poverty, and all kinds of wretchedness. And we should all work to change this.

And we can do this, motivated by love and compassion. Like Mother Teressa (sic). Or with anger and rage. Like you. And one more thing, Justin. My name is "David." What does my name mean, you ask? It means "Beloved."

David Stout,
Psychologist
Dallas, Texas

An Invocation for Mr. Stout and People Like Him in the Hopes That Their Moist Eyes Would Blind Them So They Stumble Off the Pavement Into the Path of a Beer Truck.

Dear Mr. Stout:

Thank you for giving me your bleeding heart. I promptly took it to the organ bank. They were quite pleased. I got 76 cents for it. It wasn't enough for bus fare. I walked home. When I got home, there was a message on the answering machine. It was the organ bank. They couldn't use the heart after all — it had bled itself blue. I could keep the 76 cents though, they said. So I'm sending you back your heart postage paid. Enclosed are a couple of tissues for you to wipe your eyes too. We wouldn't want your tears to blind you lest you fall off the pavement and get crushed by a truck loaded with Miller Drafts.

Because I was so excited when I received your heart, I rushed straight to the organ bank instead of writing a thank you note immediately. Where are my manners! So I am writing now to thank you for your heart and tears and to respond to your kind note.

I'm feeling much better now. I have been able to feel so much more centered and calm ever since you explained to me that the root of my oppression, the pain and the anger that I was feeling was something that I consciously chose to enjoy, like anchovies on extra cheese deep-crust pizza, boxer shorts, armpit sniffing and sadomasochism.

Also, I'm glad you so understand the racism and the marginalization that I've experienced and are able to advise me on how to deal with all these oppressions. Honestly, without you, I am nothing! I did notice all that sexual imagery in your note — all that spurting pens etc. Why, Mr. Stout, if I didn't know better, I'd think you were being quite naughty indeed!

Oh yes. How I wish I was more like Mother Theresa. Then I too could be worshiped and adored as a wrinkled colonialist. She's the last of a pure breed, you know. I'm sure there's nothing I like to do better than rescue poor sick folks and make sure they know their class and place in this world all so they can get their true reward in the glorious golden realms of heaven. (But Bless Me Father For I Have Sinned.)

Don't tell anyone this, but since you asked, I've always wanted to be an ice-pick wielding fag given to stabbing the poor hapless sap I just fucked. Oh dear, I wish I could just be satisfied with frottage, heavy kissing and foot-licking.

Oh dear me, I have to run now. Got to fire up the Norelco Wet/Dry Shaver™ so that I can keep my silky smooth hairless skin up to par. Once again, thanks so much for your kind love and compassion.

Hugs and kisses,

Justin Chin
San Francisco, California

P/S: I'll just simply die of hunger without my lacquered chopsticks! And I'm rarely seen without my slit-up-to-my-hips cheong-sam!

VI
Epilogue

When I was little, my whole family said I looked like a seal. Growing up, the image of beauty and attractiveness was always the other: the Japanese, the Korean and, especially, the Eurasian. And in my family, my brother was the good-looking one. When there was a family gathering, there would always be some remark that my brother was so damn good-looking (and his being a full-fledged yuppie corporate lawyer who lives for long weekends probably helped in their estimation). Then the gaze would turn to me and they would ask me what I was going to do with my life.

The funny thing about all this is that the last time I went home, my family said that I was beginning to look Japanese. As if that wasn't bad enough, store owners also thought I was Japanese and greetings of *Konichiwa* followed me as an enticement to enter their store. And when I did and when they found out that I was merely local, they refused to sell me an under-the-counter cheap knock-off imitation Titoni watch.

Perhaps you feel that I'm being terribly shallow, whining on and on about beauty and attractiveness. Why do we care so much about beauty and image? Why do children's stories and fairy tales tell us that good people are beautiful and bad people ugly?

But more than that, researchers have found that attractive people tend to get further in life. They found that attractive people do better in school, work, and in relationships.

In one experiment, researchers attached to an eight year old child's dismal school and test records an attractive photo of a child and to the same copy of the report, an unattractive photo of a child. Nearly twice as many of the teachers who reviewed the file recommended that the unattractive child be sent to a special education class.

In another experiment, a mediocre college-level sophomore essay (about some inane topic like "Why I Like Summer") was sent to teams of graders. To the same essay, the researchers attached photos of the supposed writer, again attractive and unattractive people. The essay with the attractive photo attached consistently received higher marks.

Researchers have found that people who think themselves unattractive are more prone to mental illness in life. In a study of 17,000 professional men, researchers found that those over six feet received a higher salary and were promoted faster.

And it's really not different in our little homo-heavens, our little gay ghettos. Perhaps it's even worse. Perhaps it's even more worse when you're coloured. Because the First Law of Homoculture states: Everyone is White, healthy, well-groomed, has pectoral muscles, is straight-acting and is "just like everyone else" unless stated otherwise. And the Second Law of Homoculture states: The bodies of those stated otherwise are "types", definable objects bound by measurable boundaries, bodies that remain at rest until a force nudges them into a constant acceleration.

It's pretty telling that one of the only four references to Asians in *The New Joy of Gay Sex*, that instruction manual for the homosexual lifestyle, that wonderful tome of homo-wisdom that no genetically-born fag should be without, should come under the heading "New Macho Image." We're told by the authors that the ACT-UP look suits all racial types as if that's really going to help us. (The other three references are found in the sections "Racism, Types" [where we learn that the slender Asian may not always want to play the shy geisha all the time and that one should make allowances for this], and "Sex With Animals" [where we learn that the Chinese are known to have "love affairs" with geese]).

The First Law of Homoculture.
The Second Law of Homoculture.

Nobody ever called me beautiful and meant it.
Nobody ever called me beautiful while they were sober.
Nobody ever called me beautiful out of bed.
Nobody ever called me beautiful without his dick in my arse.
Nobody ever called me beautiful because I'm probably not.

The First Law of Homoculture.
(feeds)
The Second Law of Homoculture.
What do you see?

(excerpts from) Go, or, The Approximate Infinite Universe of Mr. Robert Lomax

JUSTIN CHIN

1.
Robert's Lesson on How to be Tender

To be tender, you must not confuse it with weakness or sympathy. To be tender you must be meek yet strong. One of the meaning of tender is to offer, to give, to tender. To tender is tender.

The best place to start learning how to be tender is in the bedroom. When this is achieved, you may move to the bathroom, then the kitchen, following the living room and/or dining rooms, and lastly, any adjoining external spaces such as balconies, verandahs and car porches.

Tenderness can be shown while having sex, preparing meals, washing the car, drywalling, marketing, open heart surgery, kidney transplants, balancing the checkbook and even washing dishes.

To be tender, face the object that is to receive the tender and treat it as if it were a jeweled heirloom feather made of cobwebs encrusted with dust. Cobwebs are known to be the strongest threads of its diameter, but a slight careless brush will snap them, sending spiders, insect meals and dust in all directions.

2.
There are some places where dogs are afraid to bark. If a dog barks at night and no dog barks back in conversation, then the dog has seen a ghost, spirit.

3.
I am in dire need of tenderness, Robert declares one day. He looks at me as if I am supposed to do something about his dire need. All my life, I am in dire need of tenderness and I have found it with you, he declares. He smiles and places his head in my lap.

Woof.

Mr. Robert Lomax is sleeping. He is sleeping in my bed. It is early morning. I am sitting on the verandah looking out into the city. Mr. Robert Lomax has given his heart to me. I don't know what to do with it. He entreats me to be tender with it though I have no idea what I have to do to achieve that. There have to be more choices than love and tender. This I do know for sure: Some men will be loved all their lives and some men will never be loved all their lives. You know very early on which one you will be. Neither one nor the other is good nor bad, they just are. I discovered very early on which one I was to be, and I am enduring it.

Woof.

There are tourists and there are travellers. Both will go the distance, both want to see as much as possible, both are looking for adventure, both are looking for something new, both are looking for the real thing, both are willing to pay for the real thing; but one will eventually long for some semblance of home, one is already home.

And Robert? And Robert keeps asking for transfers for one more ride.

Woof.

(excerpts from) Damage

JUSTIN CHIN

1.

I was going out with this man
& he said to me,

HE SAID "why do you have to do that to your body"

& I SAID "do what"
& HE SAID "you know"

& I SAID "no, what"
& HE SAID "why do you have to sleep with all those other men"

& I SAID "well, not much I can do about that now is there"
& HE SAID "you're exactly my type but why do you have to do
that to your body"

"I wish you were really shy and bookish, you'd spend all day in the library and you'd
have big balls with big loads of cum to shoot in my mouth" HE SAID
"Well, except for the big balls and big load of cum, I can pretend, but that wouldn't be
the same would it" I SAID
"no, no, that's okay, just pretend" HE SAID.

2.

The first time I ever had sex was at the age of thirteen just before shop in the first floor
toilet of Swiss Cottage Secondary School. This man sat behind me on the bus to school
and put his foot in the crack of the seat. It was an old bus and the seats were two cushions: seat and backrest, both in a metal frame, there was a split between the two and he
pressed the tip of his shoe against me.

I glanced behind and caught his reflection in the window as the bus shuttled along a
row of trees that would darken the window enough to allow me to catch a glimpse of
him: ugly, skimpy moustache, looked like the kind of man you'd see at shopping malls
hanging out with nothing to do, the sort I'd walk across the street to avoid because he
looked like the short, tight fitting polo shirt, polyester slacks, slim gold jewellery type
that would stab you with a bearing scrapper if you looked at him wrong.

He followed me when I transferred buses and sat beside me. He apologized for touch-
ing my rear. I ignored him. After a fidgety silence, he suddenly but nervously placed his
hand on my crotch and frantically asked, pleaded, panicked for me to cover that with
my school bag, and the Adidas canvas shielded some pervert's embarrassed thrill from
the rest of the passengers.

Now when people ask, I remember it as different: He was the most gorgeous hunk, he
worked in a bank, he smelled good and we came together after he sucked me. I did not
gag on his dick. I did not nearly vomit up my breakfast from the smell of his dick. I did
not try to run out only to be grabbed from behind, slapped across the face. He did not
force his dick into my mouth while leaning over to whisper in my ear how I would get
expelled if I was caught. I was not late for class because I shitted on myself after he

tried to stick his dick into my arse without telling me. I did not spend a half hour crying in a toilet stall, cleaning myself up while praying to the Almighty Lord God Jesus Christ for forgiveness. All that did not happen: We just sucked a little, he kissed me on the mouth but I did not like it and we watched each other cum.

3.
Only I Can Fuck with my Memories:

And all those pity fucks
(Did not happen).
All those boring fucks
(Are suddenly great).
All that rough sex when I didn't want it
(Was so tender you could cry).
That incident in the restroom of the mall that made me bleed up the arse for three days
(Was the hottest sex ever).

Only I Can Fuck with my Memories and I Can't Stop There:

H. who was beaten to near death for looking too damn good in a dress
(Snapped his way out of there with so much shade, you could have put on a
shadow play).
& J. who killed himself
(Was hit by a bus like you see on Hong Kong melodramas).
& J. who died after so much pain
(Died in his sleep).
& D. who died in the hospital with no one to claim his body for weeks
(Died with all his friends around him. Someone made a joke and everybody laughed and when the laughing & repetition of the punchline died down, D. had passed away with a smile; his mother cried for months).

This is the way I know how to live and nobody has the power to fuck with my memories but me, so this body, baby, this body better play along.

Vincente Golveo

Vincente Golveo is completing a Master of Fine Arts in the Studio Art program at the University of California at Irvine. His primary medias are digital image processing and video, multimedia installation, and short experimental writing. He is working on a video about the oral histories conveyed through Filipino folk songs, various experimental multimedia projects, and is writing about new digital communication technologies from a queer and/or Asian perspective. He is co-curating a major show of contemporary works on the Filipino Diaspora scheduled for March and April of 1996 at the UC Irvine Fine Arts Gallery. He is also working on internet and multimedia projects with Visual Communications, an Asian Pacific America media center based in Los Angeles. The first project, a world wide web site for Visual Communications, premiered late May during the 1995 Asian American Film Festival in Los Angeles.

I remember what it's like to feel the sensations of being conscious, alive, sexed up, fiercely aware of the polymorphous nature of desire and its residence in my body and other bodies. These feelings are lived, perversely excessive to representation, inadequately articulated, and always in need of gratification.

I remember these feelings as the silences of my youth, growing up a gay Filipino-American. These silences now resonate for me and my queer Asian friends as a way of contesting the ideological formations of race and sexuality.

In America, representation is going digital. Desire is being harnessed at the level of the microscopic with new digital technologies. What type of fantasies do these technologies serve up? What are the politics of appearances, the tricks of light, that get people to look, to get off?

I remember as a young kid jerking off with mud. From the intense orgasms, I learned that I have bodily fluids that are part of earth. Later, much later, I learned that light, electricity, and digital technologies were invented by powerful colonizers to plunder the world from a safe distance.

Increasingly, humans interact on the level of surfaces, mediated through technologies. But when I feel my body against another body, I feel the earth as an organic rather than a colonized surface.

I like the taste of saliva on my tongue, the sticky saltiness of sweat, and the warm heat of cum running down my chest. What havoc my and my lover's fluids must do to the colonizer's ordered surfaces.

VINCENTE GOLVEO

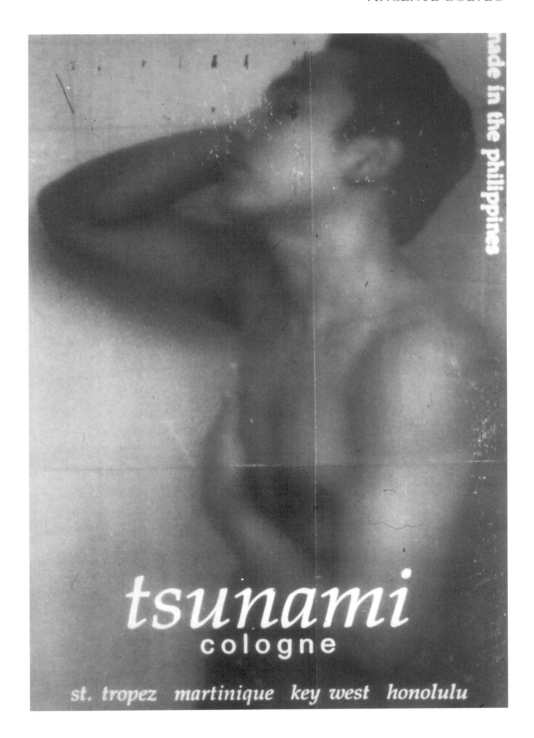

Nguyen Tan Hoang

I was born in Saigon, Vietnam, in 1971. My family and I left Vietnam by boat to Malaysia in 1979. After a year and a half in refugee camps, we arrived in the United States. I grew up in San Jose, California. I graduated with highest honors in Art and Art History at the University of California at Santa Cruz, and I am pursuing an M.F.A. in Studio Art at the University of California at Irvine. My photo-text work has been exhibited at San Francisco Camerawork, Houston Center for Photography, and Los Angeles Center for Photographic Studies. My video work has been shown at lesbian and gay film festivals in New York, San Francisco, and Los Angeles.

My photo-texts explore the homoeroticism of the Asian male body. Playing off mainstream American media representations of Asian men as computer nerds, threatening kung-fu masters, and ruthless businessmen, I employ the codes of art, fashion, advertising, and institutional pornography to situate the Asian male body in a sexual field.

While it is interesting to "include" Asian men in visual representations traditionally reserved for non-Asian/white men, it is even more important to problematize these culturally b(i)ased criteria of what constitutes hypermasculine sex appeal and strength.

This process involves questioning the structuring power of dominant modes of representation by critically and self-consciously employing different photographic discourses.

In the cologne ad series, the Asian male body takes the place of Calvin Klein's pretty white boys and girls, under exotic Oriental product names, dis-placed and in traffic between the First and Third Worlds, from Ho Chi Minh to Honolulu.

NGUYEN TAN HOANG & VINCENTE GOLVEO

NGUYEN TAN HOANG

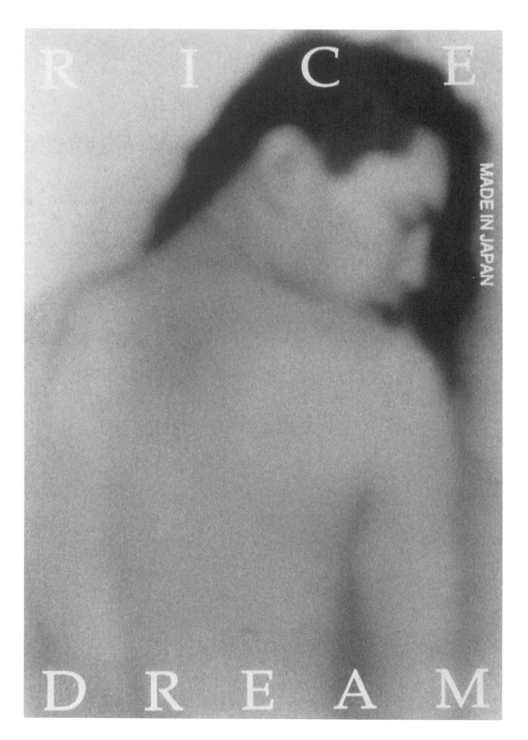

BLACK BELT
FOR MEN
FOR THE BODY

MADE IN FRANCE

FLUID BODY TALC SHAVE FOAM DEODORANT SHOWER GEL BATH SOAP

Attractive, Bi, Asian, young male, slim, athletic build, attractive figure, great body, silky-smooth, hairless, creamy & tight w/nice chest, sexy legs, juicy cock, beautiful butt. Enjoy massage, modelling, intimacy w/young handsome guys & beautiful ladies. Passionate, sensual. Discretion assured. Oriental plus.

GOM seeks well built, slim, white guys who enjoys being sucked and/or massage 16-32. Possibly developing into friendship. Phone 873-

---

GWM, 40's, healthy, French Canadian. Seeks dark-skinned native, or black boy toys with nice butts for safe sex encounters. If you like your cock, balls and ass played with, contact Drawer 2482.

Need great head? GWM seeks slim, smooth, young, horny BC Orientals, Asians, Natives, Blacks, Whites, under 25 who enjoy being sucked off and rimmed by white slim male 40. No recip expected. Contact Harv. Respond to

ORIENTAL ASIAN MALES
Best rimmer and cocksucker in Vancouver. GWM, 48, 5'11", 165, beside Stanley park. Stay here during your visit. Non-smoker, non-drinker. Let me rim and suck your asshole, balls, cock, toes, armpits and have you piss on my face and mouth. Respond to MALEBOX

RDW, I thought of you again today. **Drunk chinese**.

Indonesian/Chinese/German Biochemist would like to meet North American men & women to share life. I'm 36, bi-sexual, honest, open-minded, enjoy swimming and cycling. Since I grew up in Europe, I'd like to learn more about this continent. If you have a "normal" good character and know where you're going to, please write me a letter with photo. Everybody welcome, it is your heart and positive attitude that counts. I'll be in North America `till the end of August 1992. c/o Dr. Fennincle,

CANADIAN /CHINESE businessboy, 20's, 5'9", swimmer's build, I'm cute, funloving, straight-acting, spontaneous but safe. Seeking students or guys less than 35. Friends to start. Discretion assured. ☎ 251

SLIM BOYISH ASIAN
Very attractive WM body builder. 6', 185 lbs., blue eyes, smooth muscular body, 35. You are a young (under 25) slim Asian with a boyish appearance. This handsome, masculine WM wants to lick your smooth baby buns. No Greek.

CUTE ASIAN WANTED
Very attrac. WM, 35, masculine, smooth muscular body, a real hunk. Likes small, cute Asians. 18-25 only. Shy o.k. 621-8616. (E-10)

A fresh, young Canadian graduate from the orient, tall, slim, and good looking in feature, passionate and affectionate in heart. Would like to correspond with masculine Canadian or American white gentleman from 25 to 55 of age of the same nature. If you feel lonely or weary, why don't seek for someone who is truthful in heart. He would like to hear from you. May your heart be mingled with his tender heart. Who know one may meet each toerh in future, as the world is getting smaller. If you are sincere and serious, please write, with your photo,

HOT, SLIM ASIAN, 24, 5'6", seeks masc. top, 25-35 yrs., any race for friendship and safe hot sex. Ext. 3317

GWM SEEKS GAM ! Me: 50, silver hair, beard, passionate, stable, fun-loving, serious, seeking friend and safe sex for 1000 or 1 nites. You: 25-40 y.o.! Ext. 3496

HOT ASIAN, 22 Y.O., clean-cut, seeks masculine, collegiate types under 30 y.o. for J/o, buttplay, lite spanking and safe sex! Blond and/or heiry A+. Ext. 3506

SKINNY/SLIM 18-24 LOOK 15-19? Asian, Latino or any race, shy inexperienced OK. Fun, friendship, hot safe sex, loving expert massage, more? No smoking, alcohol, drugs. I'm very nice GWM, 50, 5'7". 155 lbs. trim mustache/beard/glasses.

LATINOS OR ASIANS, shaved butts, smooth skinned bottoms wanted by sexy, masc., hung, hairy chested GWM (SF). Ext. 3195

ASIAN SEEKS ASIAN! I am 27, 5'7", 120 lbs and I am looking for someone for friendship and/or relationship. Ext. 3214

DO YOU HAVE A BOYISH APPEARANCE? ARe you under 26 years old with a small, and very slender build? Asian, hispanic, or? I'm a WM, 32, 6', 170 lbs, brown hair/eyes, very hairy and clean shaven. Call: 597-

SEEK JAPANESE AM FRIENDS GWM wants mature, fun-loving energetic. 30-45, 5'6"+, Japanese/Japanese Americans for friendship, travel, dinner in East Bay. Be willing to commute from city to

ASIAN MALE PREFERRED But other males OK too. I'm WM 5'7½" 147, hung, disease free, don't smoke, no drugs, social drink. You: same. Any age. married OK. P/P if possible. Boxholder A,

Tall blnd, very lean, musc body, sks dominant Asian wrestler, swimmer, BB. Both late 20ish. Pin, screw & cuddle. EXT. 1427

HUNK SEEKS ASIANS FOR HOT TIMES A 30 y.o. W/M, 5'10", 160 lbs, 8", considered cute and sexy seeks hot daytime action with cute sexy Asians (any type); under 40 only. I'm a great top so if you want to get together, reply with photo to St. No. 253, SF, CA 94103. I will respond to all replies and return your photo. I guarantee total satisfaction so come and get it! (E-8)

100% TOP SEEKS HOT STEAMY RICE Asians needed to ride this studs 8" hot rod. I'm 30, 160 lbs, hairy chest and mustache. If you want to have daytime test drive reply with photo (will return) to No. 253, SF, CA 94103. Must be HIV-, (I am) Asian (any race) slender and under 40. (E-10)

HAIRY ASIANS?! Is my search an impossible one? I seek a slender Asian man with chest hair plus hairy legs and maybe facial hair. You might be Eurasian, Chinese, Japanese, Thai, Indian, under 35, well-educated, affectionate. I'm 38, slim, bearded, professional, cultured, caring. Photo/letter. Sentinel Box 8-M. (E-10)

FORTUNE COOKIE PERSONALS : WAYNE YUNG

As a gay youth, I developed a strong sense of identity, but had very little sense of gay Asian identity. I had no gay Asian friends and no awareness of gay Asian politics. It was only when I started cruising the personal ads that I glimpsed the world of gay Asian men. In an otherwise all-white gay newspaper, this was often the only proof of our existence. The personals showed us in all our diversity, beyond the negative and positive stereotypes. Most of us aren't houseboys, just as most of us aren't OG pinups. We are young and old, fat and thin, top and bottom, and everything in between. The personals let each one of us describe a unique Asian identity in forty words or less, and let each one of our admirers express a unique strain of "yellow fever." Not every rice queen wants a smooth, thin, submissive, geisha boy. I clipped out almost two hundred personals between 1991 and 1993, and built a performance around this research, called *Fortune Cookie Personals*. Looking at it today transports me to a world where everyone is Asian or wants an Asian lover. I am also reminded of the amazing diversity of identity and desire in our Asian communities. Today the newspaper personals are relatively quiet. Phone lines have replaced typeset lines, and the written culture has become an oral culture. A different medium has produced a different scene, of instant connection mediated by middle-class consumerism. Looking at these old newspaper personals, I feel a certain nostalgia for this early experiment in gay Asian "literature."

SLIM ORIENTAL MALES
who enjoy having their balls licked, their cocks sucked and their asshole kissed, licked and rimmed by a white male, 48, 5'11", 165, are strongly encouraged to write David. Vancouver. Respond to MALEBOX OC910-193 (BC)

WHERE'S TARZAN?
It's a jungle out there. A young, horny Japanese "boy" is seeking for "Tarzan" wanting to have a very hot and wild sex with "Tarzan" in the jungle. If you really loo alike "Trzan" please reply immediately with your photo of naked muscular body wearing only a loincloth and exposing you cock. Vancouver. Respond

Discreet, honest, GWM, 136 lbs, slim, smooth, good body, masculine, 38, and GOM, cute, slim, smooth, 23, wants to meet third and/or fourth similar GOM and GWM for fun exciting and safe encounters. Drawer 2557.

Masculine, attractive Asian male, professional, 28, 5'9", 150, clean cut, sincere, caring, discreet, humourous, N/S, N/D, straight lifestyle, seeks WM with matching characteristics. Lived mainly in Europe, new to Vancouver. Enjoy travel, sports, going out, arts, quiet evenings. Friendship first. Drawer 2489.

ASIAN SENSATION

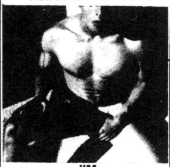

JIM
Luxurious Massage • Outcalls Only
Bpr. No. (415) 292-   Wait 3 beeps then punch in your no. (E-8)

GWM SEEKS GAM ! Me: 50, silver hair, beard, passionate, stable, fun-loving, serious, seeking friend and safe sex for 1000 or 1 nites. You: 25-40 y.o.! Ext. 3496

BM, 200 LBS, 5'10", wants Asian man with many desires. Would like to experience and service you, please let me know what you want! Ext. 3022

GOM SEEKING GWM who is sensitive and honest, to 40, for friendship and maybe more. Photo and phone number if possible. ✆ 12-12 ☎ 344

Tim McCaskell

Tim McCaskell has been active in Toronto's lesbian and gay communities since 1974 as a writer and community organizer. He was a member of The Body Politic collective from 1975 to 1986, chair of the Right To Privacy Committee's Public Action Committee from 1981-1983, founding member of the Simon Nkodi Anti-Apartheid Committee from 1986-1990 and founding member and past chair of AIDS Action Now! in 1988. He presently does work around racism, sexism and homophobia with secondary school students for the Toronto Board of Education.

In an environment where the gay community has emerged as increasingly institutionally complete, and which post-colonial patterns of immigration and diaspora have rendered increasingly multicultural, the "rice queen" has emerged alongside such other sexual categories as paedophile, masochist, sadist, transvestite, etc., and even the master categories of homosexual and heterosexual themselves. The "rice queen" displays sexual specialization and therefore categorization in a world that remains profoundly racialized. He sexualizes or eroticizes a particular racial category: "the Oriental."

Michel Foucault pointed out both the obsession of modern western society with categorizing sexualities, and also its tendency to see sexuality as the "truth" or essence of the individual.

This means that most analysis of the "rice queen" looks for an explanation in the innermost psychology of the individual and its relation to the public fantasies and discourses of imperialism and colonialism.

I argue that lust itself is impenetrable, and we will not find an explanation of the phenomenon there. The rice queen can better be explained with reference to a racialized economy produced in the sexual marketplace of the gay community and its effects on patterns of individual couplings and ultimately on individual tastes.

Towards A Sexual Economy of Rice Queenliness
Lust, Power and Racism

TIM McCASKELL

Lust

What makes you hard makes you hard. Right? It sneaks up on you. It's just there. So some white guys like Asians, which is the new code word for a "racial type" that used to be known as "oriental." (It's not where someone is from, it's the way they look that turns the crank.)

So what? Some guys like body hair, some don't. Some like blonds, some like big cocks, some like to get fucked, and some like to fuck. Some boys like boys and some like girls. So what? Lust in itself shouldn't be problematic. Gay liberation has built a movement around the respect of a range of consensual lusts.

So why do we have a category "rice queen?"

It's not a nice category. It's not said with pride. Not an honour. Not a badge to be worn proudly. Asians often distrust and dislike those known as rice queens, feeling, I suspect, that if "race" is prominently sexualized, can "racism" be far behind? Besides it's more satisfying to dump on those who are vulnerable. The white boys that won't give you a second look don't really care what you think of them.

On the other hand white gay guys often react to rice queens with the bemused indulgence that is regularly apportioned to those obsessed with some odd sexual fetish. Rice queens are often seen as losers, going for second best, unable to make it with a white guy. These are positions which reflect both the generalized racism in our society and the not so subtle rules against miscegenation that still organize many people's sex lives. (We're still supposed to stick/fuck with our "own kind.")

Even rice queens don't like rice queens. There is very little solidarity exhibited. There are lots of groups for gay Asians. There are lots of groups for Asians and friends. But can anybody think of a group for non-Asians who like Asians? For one thing rice queens are competing with each other. For another, the stigma involved means that everyone wants to show that he's not like the rest of them. Rice queenliness stands out as a practice, but it seems to be having difficulty emerging as an identity.

So smart rice queens learn to keep their mouths shut. Dumb ones, in trying to explain their lust, say dumb things. Things like, "I think I was Chinese in a past life," "They're so loyal," "They're so gentle," "It's the culture I love," "Asian culture teaches them to revere older men like me," and a range of other stereotypes that remind us cross cultural contact doesn't necessarily increase understanding.

Cross cultural contact? Half the Asians I meet are more Canadian than Molson Blue. Does the rice queen lust after culture? In spite of a tendency toward trappings of jade and apartments decorated with Chinese paintings, I think not. It is primarily the Asian body, not Asian culture which is being fetishized. The eternal question, "Where are you from? Where are you really from?" follows up a pre-existing interest in a body defined as attractive and physically inscribed as other. I think few people have been dumped because they turned out to "be" from the "wrong" country.

As for those other "explanations" of lust... Are Asians less slutty than the rest of us? I think not, not in the baths anyway. Gentle? Passive? There are as many Asian tops as bottoms and some are down right brutal. Years ago a flaky, crystal toting flower child explained to me that I was a homosexual because I was a woman in a past life. Again, I think not. Since reincarnation stories can explain everything they end up explaining nothing. It's just as likely that I was the Sultan and all these other guys were my wives.

And is it Asian culture and desire that explains why the rice queen tends to be older and the rice younger?

The answer to the riddle of the rice queen doesn't seem to lie in lust, in why somebody should find an Asian attractive. Why shouldn't he? Lust itself tends to be impenetrable. But it has something to do with why he should find so many Asians attractive. Why he moves from Asian to Asian. "So many Asians are just so damn cute," one Englishman who has since moved to Hong Kong told me.

Power

The traditional analysis of rice queenery has focused on power.It asserts that rice queens have internalized the stereotype of the exotic, erotic, passive Asian and therefore feel they can dominate. Rice queenery becomes a power trip. An extension of the Thai sex trade. An acting out of imperialist, colonialist fantasies of the sexualized orient. Doing things in the jungle you would never do at home.

Not to downplay the offensive dynamics of the sex trade. It happens. But let's face it. The sex trade is primarily organized around wealth. The racial aspect is secondary. Today the clientele is more and more likely to be wealthy Asians as westerners. Most rice queens didn't learn their stuff in Thailand. They practice in Toronto, Vancouver, Halifax, or Montreal. And Asians in Toronto, Vancouver, Halifax, and Montreal are not being driven by abject poverty into the sexual service industry. The power we're dealing with here is far more subtle.

The context for understanding the rice queen phenomenon begins with the simple volume of sexual couplings in the gay community. Straights tend to date a bit and then marry. Patterns are hard to identify. But the gay community is a sexual marketplace where people aren't so likely to get frozen with one partner. So patterns of desire in repeated couplings stand out more clearly.

Like all marketplaces, this one is fundamentally ruled by laws of supply and demand. So power is connected to attractiveness embodied in things like height and weight and age and build, as well as that constellation of physiological characteristics that our society groups together under a concept called race. Those of us who have been assigned to the category of "white" share in the benefits of a culture that has dominated the globe for the past five hundred years. Ethnocentric notions of beauty have dominated our culture and the cultures we dominated historically. Those notions continue to be reproduced both in society at large, and in the representations that market sexuality in the gay ghetto.

Those of us who have assigned other "racial" categories live with various kinds of stereotypes of otherness projected on our bodies that determine our value in the sexual marketplace, as marginal or exotic.

Back to the marketplace. Let's simplify. Consider our sexual actors as classic economic men. We have two groups. The largest is the white group, most of whom conform to the dominant ideas of beauty and lust after white guys. Most in the Asian group also conform to the dominant ideas of beauty and also lust after white guys. That means that those white guys who like Asians are in a buyers' market. We are in a position to pick and choose. While white guys that like white guys compete with all the other white guys and Asians who like white guys, the rice queen only competes against the other rice queens, and is therefore in a much better position to get what he wants, especially since the Asians are competing for him.

That's a type of power.

So where the lust first comes from is anybody's guess. But the experience of that lust puts the rice queen in a favourable situation in the sexual marketplace. And then, as my friend who went to Hong Kong said, "You get addicted to the kind of sex you get." Under these conditions, the marketplace will tend to reinforce the specialization in sexual tastes that is called the rice queen.

There is no special name for the white guy who only has sex with other white guys. That's just normal. It is always the minority that gets named first because it is the minority that requires an explanation. Names come for those who lust against the grain of this system of representations of white beauty, for whatever reasons they do it. Even the Asian who lusts against the grain and likes other Asians, has a special name, "sticky rice".

These factors also go farther to explain the age/attractiveness difference that often characterizes the rice/rice queen relationship, than any of the stereotyped references to so-called Asian culture. In a society that privileges youthful beauty, the most powerful actor will be able to choose the more beautiful, which often means the younger partner.

So the phenomenon of rice queenliness seems to have more to do with the sociology of the marketplace than with psychology or desire. It's just that lust, in this culture context, is no longer straightforward. It has implications.

Racism

As we know, power tends to corrupt. The more power you've got, the less you have to listen. The more other people will do what you want, so that they can get what they want. The more power you have, the less sensitive you have to be. In a real way rice queen/rice relations can begin to approximate gender relations. While Asians often view rice queens with the same indulgent contempt that women regularly display for men, rice queens often view Asians in a way that mimics the patronizing sexism men display for women. As one Asian man put it, "I don't mind that I turn them on, but half of them seem to want you to be their houseboy."

So finally there is racism. Our society is saturated with racist imagery, racist stereotypes, racist jokes, racist immigration laws, racist discrimination, etc., all of which contribute to that power we just talked about. So in spite of the optimistic theory that people with more interracial contact are less ethnocentric, it is the power balance in those relations that organizes how much anyone learns. The rice queen isn't necessarily less racist than the white boy that likes white boys because he has more contact. His power can insulate him from the feedback he needs to unlearn it. And the intimacy of a relationship may provide him with even more opportunities to display his racist presumptions.

The Future

So how will this finally change?

As we move deeper into the "post-colonial" epoch, the patterns of European racial dominance retreat further into the past. As economic power shifts to the Pacific Rim and new, less eurocentric ideas of beauty take their place in the increasingly integrated world media and economy, the sexual power dynamics that characterize the rice queen phenomenon are being transformed. Asians are breaking out of the stereotypes imposed by the old patterns of dominance and subservience. More Asians are attractive to more people of all "races". And the growth in self identification and Asian pride, both in Asia and especially in the diaspora, means one finds ever more young Asian gay men less enthralled with notions of white beauty. The market forces are shifting. The sexual significance of "race" is every day less saturated with the old relations of colonialism and imperialism. And when the sexual economy privileging the rice queen crumbles, so too I think will the practices of rice queenliness.

Which may lead us to the day where lust can be nothing more than unproblematic lust, requiring no explanation, requiring no "political" significance, producing no patterns to analyze. Or at least, to a whole new constellation of sexual power relationships that will make the rice queen, as we know him, unrecognizable.

Greetings

HO TAM

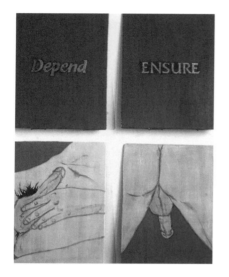

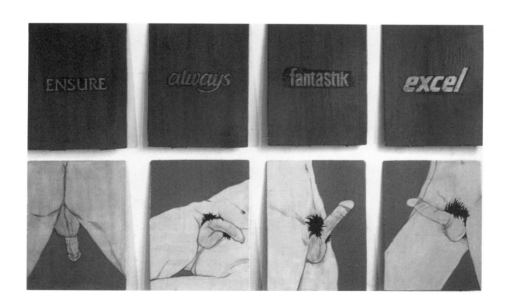

Richard Fung

Richard Fung is a Toronto-based writer and independent video producer. His videotapes include Orientations *(1984),* Chinese Characters *(1986),* Fighting Chance *(1990), and* Dirty Laundry *(1995). He is a co-founder of Gay Asians Toronto.*

Interview with Richard Fung

RICHARD FUNG

Coming Out and Producing Videos

Song: You're now 40. What was your experience of being gay and Asian back then?

Richard: I've often used that term "cultural schizophrenia" to describe the feeling of being gay and Asian. I found that coming out into a broader gay movement, I had developed a whole circle of friends and a personal infrastructure of people who were gay. I went out to gay bars, lived in a gay house, had gay friends, etc. But then I would go home to my family and have a Trinidadian and Chinese life there. And the two areas never seemed to overlap. For me, it was certainly one of the factors for being involved in a gay Asian group.

There were also very few gay Asians around in that period. You would see one or two people at the bar. You would recognize them and wonder whether it was cool to say hello or not. In fact, I remember the first time that I was able to communicate with somebody as gay and Asian. Tony Souza, Tim McCaskell and I had gone to the first Gay and Lesbian March on Washington in 1979 and there was a Third World lesbian and gay conference. Audre Lorde was the key-note speaker. I remember walking through the doors of the conference not knowing quite what to expect. This group of Asian men and women were passing and someone, who turned out to be Siong-nuar Chua (who then went on to found the gay Asian movement in Boston), came up to me and said, "The gay Asian caucus is meeting in such a such a room." Nobody had ever addressed me so unproblematically as a gay and Asian before. So that was a pretty amazing weekend and I became interested in starting a group in Toronto to recreate that incredible high.

S: How did you come to produce videos?

R: I had actually wanted to be an architect. I ended up in art school doing industrial design and I came across film by accident. Growing up in Trinidad, we were mostly exposed to Hollywood film and there was nothing that really interested me. When I was in Ireland, I saw a couple of films that affected me. One was Eric Ronmer's film *Clare's Knee* and the other one was *The Ruling Class* with Peter O'Toole. When I came to Canada, I didn't really know much about cinema but Morris Wolfe was teaching at OCA (Ontario College of Art) and I would pass by the auditorium on the way to the cafeteria and see French films, Japanese films and German films playing and I started watching them. After my first year of industrial design, I switched to film, photography and video.

My first video course was with Sylvia Spring, a feminist filmmaker. She had lived in Vancouver before she moved here and made, I think, one of the first feature films by a woman in Canada. Her course instilled in us the ethos of video as one of the tools of social change. For instance, we interviewed people in a big library strike at the University of Toronto in the late '70s.

"Looking For My Penis: Eroticizing Gay Asians"

S: Moving on to the essay "Looking for My Penis" (LFMP), how did you come to write it?

R: That's a long story. After finishing art school, I worked in community video then went back to take cinema studies and Spanish. In the meantime, John Greyson who I had known around *Centrefold* and what was later to become *Fuse*, came back from living in New York. I barely knew him but we became friends and he said I was to become a theorist. (laughs) He offered me his camcorder which I had never seen before, so we shot *Orientations*. It was going to be a discussion tool for Gay Asians of Toronto. It just kept growing and growing as a project and it got picked up for distribution which was very surprising to me. I had no idea that it would be used at all.

Then I made *Chinese Characters* as an intervention into the porn debate. This was also picked up quickly, particularly in the States and here to a lesser extent, and I found myself on the circuit. I was asked to participate in a conference that was organized by a queer reading group in New York called Bad Object Choices. They had invited well known figures like Teresa de Lauretis and Kobena Mercer to participate. As a producer, I felt a little bit awkward. I also felt I should do something on gay Asian material; but in that period, I only knew of Midi Onodera and myself.

I am not sure how I came across that body of gay porn work (for LFMP). I think it was from a friend who was working in the San Francisco porn industry. In any case, I came across the work of Sum Yung Mahn, and I decided to focus on porn.

When I made *Chinese Characters*, it was also facilitated by a group of artists working here — again John Greyson, Colin Campbell, Clive Robertson, Gary Kibbins were doing a show and asked me to join them. I mention these names because I think it's useful to show how people usually don't make things on their own but there is often a community of people who help other people. I really feel that I owe my start to other people. Some of them were gay and all of them were white. There were few people of colour working in video in Toronto then.

At that point in my community—the progressive, lefty community—there seemed to be two dominant positions on pornography. One was pro-censorship feminist position, the other, the libertarian, gay male position. There were also people like Lisa Steele, Mariana Valverde, and Chris Bearchell who were anti-censorship feminists, but a minority voice then.

One argument put a causal link between porn and rape. No distinction between gay and straight pornography was made. Anything we could do to stop pornography, including censorship, was therefore justified. On the other hand, there was the position that gay sexuality has always been censored and censured and that any critique of sexual expression was homophobic. Now, when I thought of myself in relation to these positions, I was ambivalent. On one hand, sexuality and sexual representation in porn validated my sexuality. But on the other hand, since all the images I had access to were white, I found those same images devalued me at the same time. I found my race and sexuality in a kind of conflict.

So *Chinese Characters* was meant to put forward a gay Asian critique of both dominant positions, that is pornography as good or pornography as bad. I wanted to critique porn, but without coming from a moralistic anti-sex position.

Porn figures differently in gay culture than in straight life: it's part of the bar scene, it's talked about in a more matter-of-fact way, I think. There often isn't the feeling of guilt and dirtiness that surrounds it in heterosexual life. Also, I think, even though there are certainly issues of power in porn and any kind of representation, sexual or otherwise, the fact that gender difference, the difference of power between men and women, is mainly absent in gay porn means that it's a different animal altogether. I mean, it's a related animal but different.

S: In your essay "Looking for My Penis," you write, when we look at images of gay sexual representation "it appears that the anti-racist movement has had little impact and the images of men and male beauty are still of white men and white male beauty."

R: That's still probably the case.

S: What's wrong? Why hasn't the anti-racist movement been able to change that?

R: I don't have an easy answer for this. Where there has been obvious change is in safer sex education, and in the posters that surround us in bars, baths, etc. Also in the activist press. But commercially, people print what they think will sell. Asians aren't perceived as a large enough market but perhaps this will change along with the increasing presence of Asians in the commercial film industry. And Asians have to put themselves forward too.

S: That's always a problem, having enough gay Asians volunteering for these things.

R: Right, and part of the reason for that is the way gay Asians fit into the family structure. I think so often we are held back, East Asians anyway, by notions of filial duty and what our relatives will think.

S: I see gay pornography as important because it is one of the few places where we see gay sexuality represented.

R: Yes, I think it is especially true if you look at people living in smaller cities or in rural areas, where porn might be one of the few available sources of gay validation, not to mention sexual release. I think things are changing a bit now, thank goodness. (laughs) The other day, I was channel surfing and looking at *Fashion Television* with Jeanne Beker. How many young gay men in New Brunswick or Saskatchewan get their gay validation from looking at fashion TV? There's a lot more pro lesbian and gay stuff out right now in the mainstream than before.

S: Do you envision the possibility of gay Asian porn?

R: Gay Asian North American porn? Just to make it clear, there is a large body of porn that comes out of Japan and South-East Asia but in terms of North American stuff, I haven't seen a huge amount that is interesting period. First of all, I should say that after doing all this work in porn, I don't find it that interesting anymore. I don't know if there are any gay Asian directors working in porn right now. Sure. Why not?

S: You travel around quite a bit as an artist and lecturer. What are your impressions of gay Asian communities in North America? How are they different and how are they similar?

R: In San Francisco when I first presented "Looking for My Penis," there was a lot of discussion from Asians in the audience, disagreements, etc. When I presented in other cities (and I'll leave them nameless), Asians in the audience wouldn't say a word. Then afterwards, I would be surrounded by white men asking the questions and the Asian lovers would stand in the background. So there are cultural differences from east and west for one thing. On the West Coast—of the United States at least—Asians are much more "loud mouth." (laughs) They feel they own the place.

I think there are also differences in the organizations that have developed in different cities, which are reflective of the different communities. So there are Asian-only groups or Asians and Friends groups, the friends are usually white, which colours the kinds of discussions that are possible. I wouldn't say that Asian-only groups are necessarily hunky-dory or that Asians in Asians and Friends groups are repressed. It's not that simple.

S: My impression is that in large urban American cities like San Francisco and L.A., there are more gay Asian-only groups and there seems to be a tighter gay Asian community.

R: The other thing we have to acknowledge is that the percentage of Asians who belong to gay Asian groups, either exclusive or non-exclusive, is very small relative to all the people out there, men who are attracted to, in relationships or just having sex with other men.

S: You mention in LFMP how it's relatively rare for gay Asians to date each other. Do you see that changing at all?

R: This is a very difficult one for me. For one thing, it's always striking the difference between gay Asians and Asian lesbians, because between Asian lesbians, it seems much more normal for there to be relationships with other women of colour. I see more Asian couples and I do see more couples of Asian men that are mixed race, and not with white men but with Black men or South Asians, but not a huge amount. And for me, this is a difficult thing because I am always resistant to legislating desire around relationships. But on the other hand, I think it is reflective of broader issues of desire and what is desirable. However, it is not all gay. It's interesting. I was looking at *Newsworld*, I forget what it was called "Mah-johg Orphan," something like that, there was this young Chinese-Canadian woman. She would never have a relationship with a Chinese guy. She couldn't possibly imagine it because they were too geeky and stuff. You hear this over and over again so it's not just a gay thing.

S: LFMP is considered important and empowering because it allows gay Asians to theorize and understand their relation to other people. Do you see similar work being produced?

R: Hopefully, in your book, there are other people doing that kind of work. In the States, there is the infrastructure of Asian American studies. There is no equivalent Asian Canadian studies in Canadian universities. In the States, I come across a lot of younger gay and lesbian Asians doing work in cultural studies, people who are doing masters degrees and doctorates who are beginning to publish. At the same time, I think what I have tried to do and what I would like to do is to connect issues of theory and activism. I am afraid sometimes that some of the more academic projects veer too far from the street as it were, and that's always a danger I think.

S: Do you think LFMP does that?

R: The context of the essay is an artsy, academic book. I try to avoid academic language but I can imagine it being difficult going.

I was at a conference last year and someone asked me, "What do gay Asian men want?" That's something that stuck with me for a long time. And I am not sure what the answer is. I guess for so long, I've been part of a movement, and so many of the things we wanted and that we thought we could never have, are here today. For example, just the way that lesbian and gay issues are talked about, the kind of gay representation, the fact that in Toronto we have gay city councillors and school board trustees who are out. All these kind of things that seemed impossible or unthinkable 20 years ago are here. For me, it becomes difficult to think of a new wish list. Of course, homophobia is still around and there is a huge backlash, etc., but in terms of a gay Asian agenda, it is something that needs a lot of thought.

Other Videos

S: *The Way to My Father's Village* (1988), *My Mother's Place* (1990). How did you come to work on those videos?

R: The first thing I should tell you is that this discussion is in another book Peter Steven's book *Interviews with Filmmakers*. After doing *Chinese Characters*, I found I was being turned into gay-Asian-filmmaker with hyphens in between. I thought that I just didn't want to occupy that space. I wanted other people to do that work. Not that I wasn't interested but I've always been suspicious of the way the work has been taken up. So I thought I wanted to do work that didn't deal at all with gay Asian subject matter.

I was also working more on questions of truth and documentary and being more self-reflexive. So there again, that was a logical trajectory. As I put myself more into my pieces, I also put my family and background. That's what led me into doing *The Way to My Father's Village*. At that point, my father had died and I had wanted to do a tape that dealt with questions of Asian or Chinese identification and not being from China, the question of diaspora. If I'd spent the rest of my life in Trinidad, there would not be many problems around identity, I think, because the Chinese-Trinidadian community is so specific and I am not at all strange there. But being here and actually surrounded by so many people who come from Hong Kong or China, the question of authenticity became more pressing: How Chinese am I, how West-Indian am I? All those things led me to doing the film.

S: I found those two videos interesting in their use of memory and how since you can't retrieve history, you can only reconstruct it. They're also interesting in how they critique identity. When you historicise identity, you also complicate it. So what is Chinese? What is Chinese-Trinidadian? It upsets any essential notions of identity.

R: I hope so. Privileged East Asians using the rhetoric of the Black underclass bugs me.

S: It's self-serving a lot of times.

R: It's very self-serving. It's not that class erases racism, but I think we have to find a more truthful way of talking about how race and class work. What is really annoying for me is when well-off Asians use racism to justify a simplistic nationalism and feel free to put down white people who don't have much access to power and comfort as they do. That always seems hypocritical to me. Of course, most Asians are not class privileged.

S: Well, I think the whole notion of oppression is going out of fashion.

R: But that's a problem too. There has been a huge backlash against any kind of move to social justice. So now anytime people talk about racism it's so easily dismissed through this idea of political correctness. All these critics dismiss events like Writing Thru Race (a 1994 conference in Vancouver for writers of colour and aboriginal writers), as a bunch of whiners. But if identity didn't matter, why is it mainly white guys, and mainly guys, getting to write about us? I don't know of any permanent cultural critic in a mainstream daily.

S: I think a lot of problems the anti-racist movement has experienced in the last couple of years is around the notion of identity politics. Something I experienced in Toronto with a lot of my activist friends was they made activism into an identity. So it's not like you carried out specific projects and moved on to something else, activism became its own drug.

R: God, that's such a difficult one. I completely agree with what you're saying, activism as a self-satisfied sort of life style. But I have to say that I have some problems with the construction of identity politics. I've often seen people use the critique of identity politics to dismiss attention to race, for example.

I think very often when Asians become politicized, much of our language, whether anti-racist or race nationalist, is borrowed from the African-American or African-Canadian experience. Conceptualizing a gay Asian agenda is very difficult. Homophobia, sexism, racism, and class affect us in particular ways, but we are so different ethnically and linguistically too.

S: I think there is an awareness that identity politics can be a dead end but that's not to dismiss the continued value of practicing identity politics. It is like you say, we need a more sophisticated analysis where identity, itself, is not the end.

R: I am concerned about what's going on in the international scene. There's certainly a rise in Christian, Hindu and Muslim fundamentalism with terrible results. For example, when I look at what's happening in Chechynya right now and how the West continuously disregards attacks against Muslims there or in Bosnia. This kind of indifference again produces or helps to facilitate religious fundamentalism (certainly Muslim ones) which can provide the only kind of hope in a world that doesn't care. It reenacts the Muslim Christian divide. It's not simple, as the mainstream has it, that issues of race, religion, gender, sexuality etc. are only produced by those whiners who want to manipulate the system for their own kind. I think they're being produced over and over again by the mainstream and how they treat us as different.

Round Table Discussion on Sex, Race, Desire

Ming-Yuen S. Ma is a Los Angeles-based media artist, independent curator, and educator/activist. He has created video installations, including Between The Lines: Who Speaks?, *in many North American venues. His videotapes* Aura *and* Toc Storee, *which explore different aspects of queer Asian experiences, have screened at Asian, Australian, U.S., Canadian and European festivals.*

Winston Xin was kicked out of film school, worked as a Dim Sum girl before falling into a life of magazine writing for the culturally illiterate. He is currently working on a screenplay entitled, "The Secret Life of Brent Bambary".

Wayne Yung is a writer, videomaker, performer, costume designer and sometimes towel boy, cleaning lady.

Song Cho is a "poco/pomo/homo" and probably the most educated towel boy who's ever worked at Richard's Street Service Club.

Racy Sexy

Wayne Yung, Ming-Yeun S. Ma, Winston Xin, Song Cho

Song: I think we can start from Richard Fung's essay "Looking For My Penis," judging from how often we all cite Richard. The essay was very influential in starting a critical dialogue among gay Asians about being gay and Asian. I feel, however, the essay needs to be updated in some ways. For one thing, it comes out of a very specific location which is Toronto, and out of a very specific period. The essay was published in 1988 and everything he said up to that date was quite true about how Asian men were invisibilized or fetishized. I think, however, things are rapidly changing in North America, especially in Vancouver with its large and, in many ways, prosperous Asian population.

"Blaming white guys and not doing anything about it sounds like you're expecting them to fix it somehow and white guys don't really care that much to fix it for us."

Wayne: Yeah, I think it is really a tired analysis. When I was programming for *Out on Screen* (Vancouver's queer film and video festival) this Asian fag program, I got really tired of these identity tapes where these Asian fags would go on and on about being invisible, about being fetishized and colonized by white guys and blaming everything on their white boyfriends. And that's where it

ends. Blaming white guys and not doing anything about it sounds like you're expecting them to fix it somehow and white guys don't really care that much to fix it for us. We have to do it for ourselves. In that sense, I really want to get past that analysis.

Ming: I would like to dedicate this song to…(laughter) I hate to say it but for the most part, a lot of what Richard said in his essay is still relevant. It's only been a couple of years since the essay was written and things haven't changed that much. For instance, there are porn tapes featuring two Asians having sex. But these tapes are like lesbian tapes made for straight men. You have two women having sex but they're made for a male viewer. I am working in a similar territory as Richard's essay on pornography and I don't think things have changed that much. I don't think we have such a strong voice that we can resist being placed in a marginalised position.

One of the propositions of Richard's essay is the creation of Asian-Asian eroticism. Some of us have tried to put that into practice in our lives. I think what we did was inadequate but it was still something good to do. I think there are ways to represent Asian-Asian eroticism without becoming essentialist. I think the Black equivalent of this is the discussion between Isaac Julien and Marlon Riggs. You can see from Julien's work that he's more interested in interracial eroticism and representation whereas Marlon Riggs, in his film *Tongues Untied,* considers Black men loving other Black men as the revolutionary act. At the same time, he had a white boyfriend. But there is the question of one's life and the representation one creates. I feel that I have a commitment to producing images of Asian-Asian eroticism but I don't necessarily feel like adhering to that as a policy in my life. I think those are two different things.

Winston: Coming from Toronto, where Richard lives, to Vancouver where Asians are the largest minority group, was very strange for me in that I sensed all these men, especially white men, eroticising me because I was Asian and Asians were the most eroticised minority group here. But the other side of that was, because Asians were the largest minority group, I also found a lot more Asians attracted to other Asians which I didn't see much of in Toronto. I think there is still relevance to the essay and this goes back to Wayne's point. Identity is always framed in a white context or the difference between us and whites. For example, whenever we talk about interracial relationships, it's always Asian and white. There's not as much discussion about Asian-Asian or the different kind of Asians. Asia's a big place. There's less discussion about differences of culture and background and how those things factor into a relationship. I find it much more interesting how two marginalised groups such as Asian and Black, Asian and Latino, deal with desire and identity. I am just bored of the whole us vs. white thing because I think it lends more power to them instead of empowering ourselves and our choice of desires.

Wayne: I want to comment on what Ming had to say, the necessity of in your video portraying Asian on Asian eroticism but not necessarily having that as a strict dictum in your bedroom. On one

level, I very much agree. I applaud this idea of portraying sexualities or eroticisms that don't often get portrayed, such as Asian and Asian. But for myself, I also find it really important to ground those portrayals in what's really going around me. And the reality in my life is I am sleeping with white guys right now and so that's what I portray. That's what I know and also what I think about. I guess what I really want to do is portray

> *"I am just bored of the whole us vs. white thing because I think it lends more power to them instead of empowering ourselves and our choice of desires."*

what's really going on rather than what I think should be going on which is unfortunately what I see in things like *Out* magazine where they have advertisements that look like Benetton ads, one of every colour, everyone's equal, everyone's equally empowered, and everyone has the same pec muscles and the same haircuts and the same designer t-shirts. I find that so unreal. I don't know anyone who has that kind of look, that kind of relationship to other men, and I am afraid that that kind of work hardly speaks to any of us because it's completely based on this politically-correct fantasy.

Ming: When you're making videos, you're creating a system of representation and I think lived experiences are a lot messier. I am not even sure I can figure out what some of my lived experiences mean to me. You interpret your experiences so there's never one correct or accurate portrayal of your experiences. So I think we're saying the same thing.

Song: I think Ming's accurate to point out that there are points to Richard's essay which are still accurate. I still don't see too many porns featuring Asian gay men and that is where representation lags behind reality. But what I see in Vancouver and especially along the West Coast is a critical mass of Asian cultural production where we are starting to explore our own subjectivities and not defining ourselves so much in relation to whites. I come from Toronto where issues are more polarized and you have to "pick sides." When East Tamil men are being killed by Nazi skin-heads and Black and Asian youths are harassed daily by the police, you naturally need a more activist response to protect members of your community. Unfortunately, it's also resulted in a lot of activist rhetoric of "us" of against "them" where we are homogenized as two separate camps with no hope of reconciliation. I don't think that's the case in Vancouver where Asians, as the richest minority group this country has seen, have a lot of economic power. This economic power has insulated Asians from the brunt of racism and also bought us some breathing room to start organizing culturally. Of course, not all Asians are rich either but there's still the heavy presence of Asians in Vancouver making it Canada's first Asian city, both numerically and culturally.

Wayne: When I came to Vancouver, I was quite warmed and surprised to see that white people were consuming Asian culture quite naturally. They were eating the same food we were eating. They were ordering *udon* and *ramen*, and they

knew what they were ordering. They weren't just ordering sweet and sour chicken balls like they do back in the prairies where I am from. In the gay scene as well, there's a lot more mixing whereas back home, there is still a great deal of racial segregation.

Winston: I think Song, you might have a point that we have economic power. But if you look at who really has power in this city, they're still white. So who really has the power? I also think if there's no incentive to using that economic power towards any political or cultural ends, it doesn't do anything. It goes to flipping real estate and that's about it. I really don't agree with that whole economic thing. I think that's one thing whites use to discriminate against Asians, particularly Hong Kong Chinese. "Oh, they're buying up all the condos. They're buying up the land, blah, blah, blah..." I think the people who really make this economy move are still white.

As far as I know from growing up in Hong Kong, the conditions of immigration to U.S., Australia and Canada are economically determined—i.e., you have to bring a certain amount of money with you when you come. However, due to different licensing requirements, many professionals from Asia come here but can't practice. So they bring the capital but don't really have economic power. In fact, many immigrants have to live on the money they bring over since they can't work here.

Ming: One thing we should also note about pornography is that we might not necessarily get off looking at people of our own race have sex. Pornography is about fantasy. You might not even find your preferred practice a turn-on for all you know. So it's not so much of this equation issue. When you talk about representation, it's very, very fluid and it's very individual which makes it interesting for me as a filmmaker.

Wayne: I agree with Ming's point that just putting more Asian faces into porn isn't necessarily going to make porn something I want to consume. That goes back to Richard's point in his essay, that regardless of whose faces are on the screen, most or almost all of the production is geared towards a white audience. They still don't pay attention or ask what an Asian audience would like to see. Myself, as a potato queen, or at least right now as a potato queen, I would really be interested in seeing gay white men on screen who somehow expressed desire for Asian men but in a way that would turn me on as an Asian. That would mean a guy who wasn't into dominating me or making me submissive or stereotyping me basically. That could be sexy too, true, but I guess the only way to get around that is to have producers, writers and directors create the porn they would want to see as gay Asian men.

Winston: What I find interesting in this discussion about desire and pornography is, why is it that Asian men have a hard time eroticising other Asian men when whites don't have a problem eroticising other whites or Asians? There are Asian porn magazines out there but people who buy it are probably mostly white.

Ming: Gay porn in Japan is produced for an Asian audience.

Wayne: But that's for an Asian audience in Asia, right? I am not like an Asian in Asia. My desires come from being born and raised here in Canada. That's again something Richard Fung talks about (again Richard Fung!) in the Q & A

attached to the essay. People keep telling him, if you want Asian representation, why don't you just get some tapes from Thailand, some tapes from Japan because they're full of that stuff and Richard responds, but he didn't grow up there. That's not his cultural context, that's not his upbringing. That's my problem as well. I can't relate to stuff in Asia anymore than any other person born in Canada can.

Winston: A lot of Asians, it seems, explain their desire for white men by saying it's because they were brought up in this culture. What I find interesting is how did white men break away from that and start eroticising other groups? Is it as simplistic as the attraction to the other thing? I don't buy that. I am still bewildered when I meet a white guy from a rural area and he has formed this desire for Asians. We often use the excuse, "Well, we're attracted to white guys because that's all we see on TV or porn." It's interesting how they formulated their specific desires.

Song: I think it's because we collapse a lot of issues into race. I know for myself, part of what motivates my desire is not only the race but also the class position of the person that I am seeing. For the longest time, I was and still am, to a certain extent, aspiring to middle-classness. So it was important for me to date someone from the middle-class to feel I was "moving up." In Vancouver, I also find myself eroticising other Asians. But when I use the term Asian, I really mean Korean and Japanese. Those are the two groups of Asians that I find myself time and time again attracted to. The Japanese that I meet in Vancouver tend to be much more middle-class and Westernized than any other Asian group, including Koreans, so I am attracted to that. They also tend to have the body type that I am attracted to which is slightly larger than mine and muscular. So it's a combination of things: class, body type and culture that inform my desire. The other thing is the position Japan has occupied in Asia, especially in relation to Korea, as an imperial power. If I put my desire within that historical context, again it's in terms of the oppressed desiring the oppressor, even though I don't believe that's quite it.

Wayne: That's the observation that I had about my desire. When I was growing up in Edmonton, I never got attracted to another Asian guy and I thought it might have to do with race. But then I came to another conclusion that was about not really wanting to question that desire because trying to analyze and question my preference for a certain race was like trying to question my preference for a certain gender and I get tired of trying to second-guess what makes me hard. But anyways, when I came to Vancouver, I was exposed to a much wider variety of Asian men and I started being very rarely, very occasionally attracted to other Asian guys. I found that the kind of guys who were attracting me were the kind of guys I would never meet in Edmonton: guys who were very self-confident about their sexuality, very secure in their identity, very "Western" in their aggressiveness and forwardness (laughter), and I say Western in the sense that white people here grow up feeling confident about their race 'cause in my city, Asians who grow up in Edmonton grow up feeling very unconfident, feeling you should shut up, you shouldn't talk too loud, you should hide in the corner, you shouldn't be too aggressive, you shouldn't be too noticeable, you shouldn't be too expressive and you shouldn't be too forward. I found then maybe, I wasn't attracted to them not because of their skin colour but because they had been so oppressed I found them boring!

Song: I think the reason I am able to be attracted to other Asians in Vancouver is because there's the context where Asian-Asian relationships are affirmed. I spent five years in Ottawa which is a very white city, typically middle-class, bureaucratic, with a large civil servant population. In Ottawa, if I were to have dated other Asians, I would have felt doubly marginalised. In Ottawa, I saw whites as "jitters," as people who could legitimize my presence in gay bars and clubs. In Vancouver, I don't need that same sense of reassurance. Because there are so many Asian groups represented in Vancouver, I also don't necessarily see other Asians as just "Asians." I see them as individuals with personal differences like everyone else.

Winston: Maybe if there were more Asians out there in porn, that would also create a space for eroticising other Asians.

Song: Working in a men's sauna, I also tend to consume a lot of porn especially from the L.A. porn industry. These are the ones with tanned white guys but with bums that are always white to highlight their whiteness. I view a lot of these porn as white-supremacist in the way they eroticise white bodies as *white* bodies. I don't think these videos are necessarily racist just because they're all white. What I find offensive is the way they highlight that whiteness to signify both privilege and desirability.

Ming: I have an exposé. A lot of people who work in the L.A. porn industry are Asian.

Wayne: That still doesn't address whether or not these tapes are being made for an Asian audience.
Ming: We often paint this picture that there's this monolithic group of white men making porn for themselves and I

don't think that's true. But it's still produced for white guys, I guess.

Song: A problem I have with this type of conversation is that we reduce politics to individuals and whether they have good or bad intentions. When I talk about porn, I am not particularly concerned about who is exactly producing this stuff. An Asian could be making it and it wouldn't necessarily make any difference. I am more concerned about how these images buy into and reinforce the ideology of white as beautiful while denigrating everything else.

Wayne: This is true. This is where I got a lot of my potato queenliness. So it may be necessary to produce other kinds of images to be consumed by people. But, on the other hand, I still want images that turn me on. And if I happen to be turned on by white guys, I'll like to see that porn. However, I'll like to see that produced by Asian producers who are sensitive to the ways Asian guys could be turned on by images of white men.

Ming: I don't think there's inherently a better system of representation. The question at hand for me is more about an image culture than positive or negative images. We don't live in a vacuum but in cultural spaces that are, if anything, saturated with images. At this point, it is more worthwhile for me to create resistant subject positions from which these images can be re-interpreted or re-claimed.

Wayne: That would imply another strategy which is not about finding Asian gay producers to make the tapes but to educate the audience to subvert the readings of the tapes that presently exist.

Ming: I would challenge the notion that there is a singular gay Asian subject position.

Song: As Wayne put it in his program note for *Out on Screen*, Asian gay culture is something that is distinctively different from both the gay white mainstream and the straight Asian mainstream. I would define Asian gay culture as not one or the other, something that still needs to be created and which respects differences among gay Asians.

Wayne: Gay Asian culture is very fluid.

Winston: This goes way back to Wayne's thing about how gay Asians tend to be obedient, submissive, quiet etc. I tend to be not like that. I used to wonder, "Hey, is it because I am really Westernized?" But when you go to a Cantonese restaurant and see see all the ruckus as people try to grab the bill, I realize, I am really outspoken and I don't follow the stereotypes not because I am so Westernized as I am really Cantonese. (laughter)

Wayne: When I said Westernized, I really think I chose the wrong word. What I really mean is unrepressed, unselfrepressed.

Winston: Ming, you grew up in Hong Kong until you were fifteen. So your desire for men were for other Chinese?

Ming: Well, Hong Kong is a colony, albeit a very successful colony. It's a very unique case that the Chinese there have quite a bit of power. Still, when it comes down to it, they are still being fucked over both by the Chinese government and Britain. Growing up in the colony, you still had to deal with Eurocentric ideals but that was countered by the mass of Asians whom you see everyday. My first boyfriend was Chinese. I don't have a problem eroticising other Asians. My problem with other Asians arises more from my occupation as an artist and my politics. It comes down to where you live, the clothes you wear, where you hang out.

Wayne: I would like to explore more what Ming is talking about, the position of gay Asian artists, videomakers and writers in the context of the gay Asian community in North America. I, myself, as an artist find that quite often the gay Asian community here, on one hand, supports me because they feel that it's this great Benetton thing. I am representing everybody and I am giving us visibility. On the other hand, they shun me because I have little money and I don't really aspire to all the yuppie goals that they're aspiring to. I don't have a condo, I don't have real-estate, and I am also not adverse to challenging their bougie desires.

Ming: I have a very precarious relationship with visible gay Asians who are basically organized around groups. I live in L.A. and I really don't have dialogue with the local gay Asian groups primarily because they're really not interested in what I am doing. I think they're much more geared to more mainstream expression, such as Hollywood feature films, and the people who I hang around with are artists who might or might not be gay and Asian. But I guess I have to contextualize this by saying that I came from a background of community organizing through a couple of gay Asian groups like the one in New York, and their support was really important when I first started making work. I am at this point where I feel like I don't necessarily speak only to gay Asians. I don't think there is a monolithic gay Asian audience. I think the community is too diverse for that. But at the same time, I wouldn't be upset if everyone in the audience was gay and Asian. That's cool too. I deal with issues that I need to deal with and if that coincides with what that particular community is interested in, that's great, but if

not, that's okay too. This is coming from a whole history of being involved with various communities.

Wayne: I found GAVA (Gay Asians of Vancouver Area) supportive but at an arms-length support which is probably the best and only way to do it. They figure, "Oh, there's Wayne going and doing another one of his weird things but because he's gay and Asian and he's a nice guy..." They like me on a personal level but quite often, they disagree with my work but they're too polite to say that they disagree with my work. A note on what Ming said about audience: I agree that it's a very ambiguous thing to aim for a gay Asian audience when it's really a myth that there can be this gay Asian audience that you can count on and you know what their response is gonna be etc. But for me, the ambiguity comes when a lot of programmers are completely unconscious that there is a racial diversity in the audience. A lot of programmers assume that the audience is all white and as such, shares set of common, North American, white experiences. For example, going to Sunday school. When they start talking about that Christian stuff, I don't know what they're talking about because I've never been to that stuff. There's a really large set of stuff that they assume that those of us who aren't white also understand. As a curator for *Out on Screen*, I am doing this experiment where I am assuming everyone in the audience understands gay Asian identity politics and it'll be interesting to see what happens when all those white boys show up.

Winston: How do I relate to the mainstream gay Asian community? Well, I am poor, I don't have a car, I don't have a decent job. I don't aspire to being a businessman or a doctor, and I don't know know how to order eloquently during dim sum and I can't sing karaoke songs so I guess that's how I relate. But some of my best friends are gay and Asian. (laughter) When I was in detox overcoming my heroine addiction, the doctor who examined me was a Chinese physician and he brought up this point that I was the only second Asian that they'd ever seen in detox, implying that I was not a good Asian. For some Asians who come to this country, there is the sense that they have to prove themselves economically to the predominantly white society, to save face, so to speak. For Asians who don't fit the mould, we're seen as bad Asians. We're making them lose face.

Wayne: It really strikes on certain insecurities as well about feeling inadequate in a white-dominated culture that we have to overachieve intellectually and economically, so that when someone like Winston shows up and is a slacker at this condo party, it kind of threatens everyone's values about what you should be doing with your life.

Ming: What I notice in U.S. is the hunger for "bad" Asian images: John Moritsugu, Gregg Araki. In my experience working for film festivals, the "bad" Asian shows are the popular shows. You're also talking about San Francisco and Los Angeles where you have third- or fourth-generation Asian-Americans whose consciousness of racial politics is very much derived from the civil rights movement as opposed to immigrant-based politics. Their thing is Asians are boring and nerdy.

Wayne: I think a lot of the gay Asian community's attitudes are shaped by immigrant attitudes and immigrant politics that are very different from what you were saying about third-generation amd fourth-generation Americans. For example, GAVA is very much based on the idea of providing a safe space for gay Asians and safe space implying that they're mostly immigrant gay Asians who feel threatened or insecure so certain subjects can't be talked about and certain people aren't invited like really aggressive rice queens. I find for myself, I feel silenced because I can't talk about these really confrontational things like questioning how we chase white boyfriends because it threatens the safe space at GAVA.

Winston: They never talk about that?

Wayne: No, they just chase them!

Ming: That's interesting because I find that in the American gay Asian groups, the party line is Asians go out with other Asians because that's the empowering thing to do.

Wayne: I think that's a really interesting point about Asian on Asian being politically correct. In the straight immigrant community, there is strong pressure to stay within your race and to marry a spouse who is of your race and cultural background. Now, why is it that gay Asian men don't respond in the same way to that kind of pressure to keep it within the culture?

Song: I think that's because we have to go out into a predominantly white gay community to find sex and partners.

Ming: I think there are two models of Asian/Asian relationships. One is first-generation immigrants who feel comfortable with people who speak the same language and have the same cultural background. The other is Asian-Americans who go out with other Asians or make an effort to do so because of their politics.

Wayne: What you say about the first position also holds here. There is also a very invisible subculture of very recent Asians, not immigrants so much as tourists or exchange students who're

> "...in the American gay Asian groups, the party line is Asians go out with other Asians because that's the empowering thing to do."

here for only a few months, who never pick up enough English to hang around GAVA or at the gay bars. So there's these little clatches of Cantonese speaking gay people who call each other up and go to dim sum and stuff. I went to one of these little groups by accident somehow. God knows how I got involved because the whole conversation was going on in Cantonese and I was just sitting there like a log. But I know a lot of the conversation was about how they felt completely invisible here because they couldn't interact with the English-speaking community even at GAVA which purported to provide a safe space.

Song: Going back to this book, the fact that it's entirely written in English says a lot about our specific location as Asians living and working in North America.

Wayne: On a grassroots level, Song and I've been developing the slang part of our culture. Once I watched on television of two Black fags doing slang and I was really, really impressed to see them expressing a culture that was partly derived from gay white slang but also from a black, hip-hop street culture so it was a unique hybrid of the two. So Song and I had been playing around with this idea and one of the things we've decided to appropriate is the term "yellow cab."

Song: All my Japanese girlfriends know this term. It's what white guys call Japanese girls because they're "easy to pick up." The term is useful for pointing out how we, as gay Asian men, are also perceived as being more available for white gay consumption.

VINCENTE GOLVEO

It's all a matter of economics.

Here there is a better life.

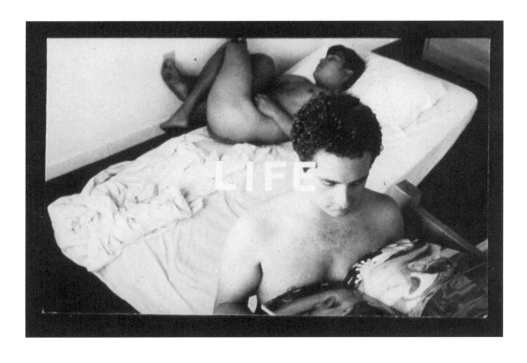

Chi-Wai Au

I was born in Hong Kong in 1972 and raised in Los Angeles. I received my B.A. from Pomona College and now teach in the public schools in Los Angeles. My poetry has recently appeared in The Asian Pacific American Journal.

Destinations

CHI-WAI AU

I see questions brooding
and riding past your head,
how they run into difficult stops.
In the cradle of my arms,
you concede no stranger love
than this, the daring reflection
of your brown eyes in mine
shaped like the muted hunger
of mouths.

In the moments when we peer
into our cracked, separate lives,
we see the destinations we choose
are long and slow in approaching,
no directions to mark the way.
If you're left standing to guess
at the crossings of the wind,
lost in white dust and light,
here's my answer for you,
here's where, I believe,
our wanderings must begin:

Let my arms pull close your waist,
let these two palms go down
the hard length of your back,
our naked bodies becoming, you see,
the only maps we need to follow
in the darkened space of our beds.

Blue Light

CHI-WAI AU

Hold his shoulders and move into him.
This time, your hands will
break from their bondage,
a pair of thieves stealing from
his body behind shut doors.

Gone the hour of beaten silence,
invisible ropes that possessed you,
you trace your fingers through
the sweat of his legs and hardened body,
closing your teeth over his hair.

When he stretches his
arms to receive you,
you turn lawless. You lower
yourself to your knees
to cry under the room's blue light,

For what is there before you,
as your mouth runs free
with the shameless taste of salt,
as your whispers vanish together
quickly into the low, open night?

The Bachelor Son

CHI-WAI AU

I view the positions they take,
she on the right, he on the left,
when we sit for the evening

meal. Their yellow ivory
chopsticks fish the table,
arranging food for my plate.

There's the chicken, round,
bought at the poultry market,
the careful soup boiled

in the large, clay pot.
Swollen, black mushrooms
cover a dish of greens,

and I show the favorable,
eat with double courtesy.
On this occasion home,

delicate hunters want my
life. Shall I serve them both,
stone lions, set before me?

School Portraits

CHI-WAI AU

Jeff Lee and I got to be
best friends at Northpark Junior High.
Bored during fourth period English,
we traded Chinese in whispers
and slipped notes and chewing gum
across our tables in the back. Lunchtime,
we munched on plain ham sandwiches and
followed the basketball games on the blacktop.

Mother worked afternoons at the restaurant
and Jeff walked home after school with me.
We watched television in her room upstairs,
our stomachs thrown flat on the sagging bed.
I remember the first day of gym class,
we'd laughed and poked each other in the chest.
We were pulling off our maroon and gray shorts
and stripping the tee-shirts from our skinny backs.

It was the seventh grade and I remember
how I was thirteen, really clumsy with most things.
Like algebra assignments, like that new year,
the tender stirring of my first boyish love.

Bird's Nest Soup (Lines on AIDS)

CHI-WAI AU

Haizi, I'm an old woman and heaven
no longer has any eyes.
For weeks I've watched this fever
waste pounds of your flesh away.
Tell me, who will help me swallow
this difficult lump of grief?

Today I make busy in the kitchen
and ready this excellent broth for you.
Costly ingredients kept for this pot,
I mix in the dried spit of swallows,
the soft breast of a young hen.
I bring the bowl to your bed,

such delicate flavors I've stirred in:
Dear son, does your mouth taste the salt
shaken from this cup of tears?
Do your lips discern
the bitterness, fine extract,
taken from my swollen heart?

Chen Lin

I recently graduated from the Masters of Professional Writing program at the University of Southern California, and will be finishing my thesis in August. My thesis will be a collection of short stories. I've done readings in Los Angeles and at University of California, Riverside where I did my undergraduate work.

I was born in Taipei, Taiwan and grew up in southern California. In much of my work, I explore (and exploit) the distance between and melding of language. "Being fluent" in a mother-tongue and/or an adopted language; in the language of camp and of coming-out; and in the silences in which we communicate the most clearly: all of this is what interests and frustrates me most.

Word Choices

CHEN LIN

This is a story about a young Taiwanese American and his father. At home the young man speaks a mixture of English and Taiwanese, although he speaks more English than Taiwanese. His father understands enough English to get by.

The young man's father has been asking him about girlfriends. He answers by smiling bashfully and changing the subject. The father doesn't understand. His son has many female friends, but no girlfriend? He periodically asks his question in different ways, but the son's answer is always the same.

What's been taken as bashfulness is actually embarrassment and frustration. The young man decides one day that he must confront his father and tell.

Not knowing the Taiwanese words, the son says to his father, "Papa, I am gay."

After a moment of silence, the father answers in his thick accent, "Really?"

Wait. That doesn't read right. I delete it and try again.

"Papa, I am gay."

After a moment of silence, the father answers in his thick accent, "Leelly?"

Ugh. That's even worse. I try again.

"Papa, I am gay."

After a moment of silence, the father answers in Taiwanese, "Really?"

After a moment of silence, the father answers, "Gumannei?"

That doesn't look right. There's no system of Romanizing Taiwanese, no one would know what that's supposed to say.

After a moment of silence, the father answers, "Zun-te?"

No, that's not Taiwanese, that's Mandarin. Besides, I'm not even sure the ping-ying is correct.

I re-read what I have.

Not knowing the Taiwanese words, the son says to his father, "Papa, I am gay."

I'm stuck. What does the father say? How does he say it?

Not knowing the Taiwanese words, the son says to his father, "Papa, I am gay."

His father looks down and says nothing.

A Secret Language

CHEN LIN

It's after dinner and we're watching *Breakfast in Tokyo* on the International Channel. My father and older brother are relaxing in the living room. I'm in the kitchen washing dishes, but I can see the TV from here. Mother died years ago and it's just us guys at home, so there's no question who inherited her chores: Me, the youngest.

Father translates bits and pieces of the tv show from Japanese to Taiwanese for Brother and me; Taiwanese because his English is limited. I remember how he and Mother used to speak Japanese whenever they needed to talk freely but didn't want us kids to know what they were discussing. Their own secret language. How I envy that! Ironically, during the Japanese Occupation, Taiwanese was the secret language. A shameful thing, it was used only when necessary and in whispers, around the house, in tight huddles. If caught, the transgressors would be beaten, their homes ransacked for evidence of dissension.

A sleepy-faced woman is on TV making breakfast for her husband and children who are still snoozing. She smiles and bows perfunctorily at the camera which keeps getting in her way. Her tired, pinched eyes show just a glimmer of annoyance which makes me think that the show's host and camera-men barged in on her without warning. How rude, if that's what's happened. But I don't know. Father doesn't say.

The phone rings. I rinse the suds from my hands and answer it. It's my friend.

"Hey girl! We're going dancing tonight. Can you come?"

"Sure! What time?" I ask discreetly.

A group of Japanese drag-queens, gathered around a table inside a cabaret, sit posing in their seats, waiting to be served.

"Hey! Drag-queens!" I talk about them loudly on the phone, describing them gloriously, laugh at their grand gestures, and stare at the back of Brother's head knowing he can hear me.

Even though I'm speaking excitedly, I'm careful about my words. I'm not out to him yet. The strategy is to feed him full of hints and suggestions until he bursts out asking. Or I'll tell him when the time is right. Either way he won't be able to say that he didn't have a clue.

Father can hear, but I doubt he understands. My slang-slick English is to him as Japanese is to me.

My brother is shocked at how beautiful the drag-queens are, how convincing. He asks Father if they're performers at the cabaret, or just customers.

"Performers, yes. They are women-born-as-men," Father says.

Brother doesn't respond, just quietly receives the answer. Perhaps he's been piecing together my suggestions, like the "performance" I just gave over the phone, and feels uncomfortable acknowledging Father's response. Wishful thinking. I hang up, finish the dishes, and go to the living room to watch the show. Plenty of time to shower and dress before going out.

We watch a bride-to-be who is too nervous to eat on the morning of her wedding day. Father sucks his teeth and belches. "What kind of girl will you marry?" he asks me.

Why is he asking me that? Why now after my excited outburst about drag-queens? Did I let something slip, something perhaps non-verbal? Did I queen-out?

Brother answers, "He'll probably bring home a black girl."

I laugh. Not at the idea of marrying a black girl, but because of the subtle suggestion that I am different, that I will not fulfill Father's expectations.

"Marry a good girl," Father instructs. "Someone who will cook and clean, take care of you."

I shake my head. "I'll marry a princess."

The Space Between Breaths

CHEN LIN

The longest period of time that Papa has stopped breathing while asleep is nine seconds. The condition is called sleep apnea, and most people who have it don't know that they've got it. They have to be told, usually by a worried and sleepless spouse. Since my mother is dead, that responsibility rests on me. I haven't told him yet. I don't think I will. I can imagine him worrying so much about not breathing that he'd develop insomnia, and lying around quietly all night long trying to fall asleep is much more stressful than getting up in the morning sluggish and grouchy.

His snoring sounds live waves at the beach: a roar coming in, and a soft, breathy hiss going out. This rhythm is sometimes followed by a silence which is later broken by a loud snort and him turning over in bed and/or coughing to clear whatever went down the wrong tube. This is what I listen for when I'm awake in my room.

The first night Matt spent at the house, he asked how I could sleep with all the noise. Matt snores too. "It's like you go deaf once you're asleep, Peter," he observed. I told him he's lucky that I'm such a sound sleeper, and he agreed. Smart guy.

That was two weeks after the Northridge quake. I moved home because my apartment building got red-tagged and had to be cleared in two days. There were cracks in the walls that you could literally stick your whole hand into. Even though I'd gone home, I lived out of boxes. Why unpack completely if I was just going to find another apartment? So I kept some boxes in the garage, but most of them were in my room for easy access to things I needed, like clothes. They were stacked up against the wall between Papa's bedroom and mine. I could still hear his snoring though.

Matt asked if I wanted to stay with him while we were packing my stuff. I told him it would be easier if I went home: I could stay as along as I wanted and save money while looking for a new place. Then, after I had already turned him down, I wanted to say yes. It would've been an excuse not to go back home. But, I kept quiet. If my first impulse was to say no, that must have meant something.

The first thing I did, the night I came home, was straighten up my bookshelves. Papa stood in the doorway watching me work and asked how the quake was Downtown. I didn't remember, I was so scared. What I did remember was being wide awake five minutes before the earthquake, but I didn't have the instincts to dive under a table or run outside like a dog would have done. Instead, I rolled over on my stomach and tried to go back to sleep. Then the quake hit and I was paralyzed.

"Inertia," I said over my shoulder.

Papa asked what that meant. I told him it's when you don't move for such a long time that you just don't want to anymore. He nodded, then shook his head.

"All animals have instinct." He tapped his sternum to emphasize his words. Then he tapped the side of his head as if to suggest that I think something through. "People just don't listen. In the wild, no choice. Sharks must swim or drown."

That was something I had translated for him from a nature show we watched together. Large sharks, such as the Great White, must constantly swim in order to pass enough oxygenated water through their gills, otherwise they'd drown. I remember being amazed that these powerful creatures could have such a simple yet deadly flaw. But now that Papa has turned the fact into an aphorism, I felt like a kid being lectured.

I quieted the side of me that wanted to refute him, to make a joke, to have the last word, so I nodded and continued restacking books.

He yawned, loudly. I turned to ask if he was going to bed. He let out his gulp of air and smacked his lips. With the ends of his white mustache curling down around his dark, thin mouth, he looked like a catfish. "Good night. I'm playing mah-johg early tomorrow. Put your boxes in the garage. Get some sleep."

I telephoned Matt after Papa was soundly snoring. He had discovered a crack in the wall opposite his bed, just above his television set. I told him my books jumped off the shelves. He wanted me to go over, to spend the night. I asked him to come here. His place had more privacy. I agreed. So would I go over? I told him to wait a couple days until Friday when we'd have the whole weekend.

Early Friday evening I told Papa that I was going camping for the weekend with my friend, Matt. He doesn't know we're lovers and I don't plan on telling him. Not now anyway. I told him we'd be leaving early Saturday morning so I'd be spending the night at his apartment. He reminded me to pack warm clothes and to get rid of the boxes in my room before I left. I threw a sweater around my shoulders and took off thinking the boxes could wait.

Matt rented movies and we stayed in all weekend. He did all the cooking. He actually enjoys it, which is good because I don't. I did the dishes. We were a picture of domesticity: me washing dishes in the sink, Matt plastic-wrapping the leftover chicken and pasta. For a Chinese boy he makes better Italian than rice or noodles. He's thankful that I'm not a picky eater. I'm thankful that he cooks.

"It's easier to look for a place out here if you stay, Peter," Matt suggested later when we were in bed. I clicked off the TV and stroked his soft black hair. He moved his head off my shoulder and kissed my chest. The crack on the wall was more pronounced than he made it seem over the phone. It split the plaster like a black bolt of lightning angling down above the TV. I stared at the cracked wall as images of us doing mundane things together flashed across my mind: me pushing a grocery cart and him checking his list; weekly laundry at the laundromat; sitting silently on the couch watching TV. It all seemed so normal. So static. I kissed the top of his head.

"I'll find a place soon."

Matt would spend a night or two during the week when I still had my apartment downtown, or I'd go to his place. I missed being able to see him whenever I wanted. The only times that we wouldn't see each other was on weekends when I'd come home to visit Papa. We'd make up the lost weekend during the week.

Papa doesn't do much on weekdays. Usually he's in the garden weeding the rows of strawberry and scallion. Once or twice a week he'd get a mah-johg call and would be gone all day and all night and wouldn't come home until two or three in the morning. He has all the stamina in the world for mah-johg.

During one of these mah-johg nights, Matt and I tried phone sex. We spoke in deep, breathy voices and made noises we didn't normally make. In the middle of laughing hysterically, Matt became silent. A second later, the ground rumbled and the house shook. I held my breath. When the rattling stopped, the sudden stillness roared in my ears like an undersea current, enveloping, distant. I looked at the receiver clenched in my fist, and for a moment forgot what I was doing with it.

"Hello?"

"You rock my world," Matt said. I didn't laugh. I wanted to see him. I asked him to come over even though I knew he couldn't. I offered to wake him early or he could call in sick, one sick-day wouldn't cost him his job. He wished he could. "We'll see each other this weekend," he said. Could he come here? There was a long pause before he said yes. Promise? Yes. We hung up. I lay in bed, clutching my pillow, and didn't relax until I heard Papa come home at around two. I stayed awake until his rhythmic snoring coming through the wall lulled me to sleep.

As promised, Matt came over Saturday and we went out. We hung around Old Town Pasadena because of the freeway closures in Westside and all the surface traffic there. We came back after Papa was asleep. In the morning, I told Papa that it was too late after the movie for Matt to drive home so he stayed here.

This was the second time in four weeks that Matt has spent the night. Perhaps the familiarity was what prompted Papa to insist on the two of us staying home for brunch. He cooked a large pot of noodles with shrimp and vegetables, and warmed leftover spicy pork loin in the microwave. Matt watched intently as he chopped and stirred, hoping to learn some tricks.

During brunch, Papa asked if we had felt the earthquake on Wednesday night, the night Matt and I were on the phone. I corrected him saying that it was an aftershock: earthquakes were caused by volcanic activity or by the earth's plates pushing or rubbing together, and aftershocks were the release of built-up pressure left over from the quake. Papa wasn't impressed. He'd seen the same TV show.

"You play mah-johg, Matt?" he asked.

Matt looked a little embarrassed. "No, I never learned. Mom and Dad don't play."

"Your father and mother don't play? What kind of Chinese is that?"

"They never learned, either. They were born here."

Papa nodded gravely. "Mah-johg is good, exercises the mind. Keeps the brain young." He tapped the side of his head with a finger. "Get old in here, you die fast."

I began clearing the table and Matt got up to help. He took Papa's bowl and chopsticks from him.

"We'll clean up Mr. Wu. You've been so busy cooking."

"Okay!" Papa answered enthusiastically. He yawned and stretched in his seat but didn't leave the table. He looked happy but tired. Probably had a fitful night. Apnea does that, makes you lose sleep.

I washed the dishes and Matt dried while fetching questions from Papa about being a Chinese boy born and raised in America. Did they watch Chinese TV shows at home? He explained that he lived on his own and no, he didn't watch Chinese television. Has he visited China yet? No, but hopefully someday. Would he most likely marry a white girl? Matt flicked some suds at me. No, not likely. Papa sat there nodding and sucking his teeth. I ignored the bubbles melting on my shirt.

"This one," Papa said about me. "So Americanized. I don't know. Maybe, I think, he will marry a white girl." Matt elbowed me when I had a bowl in my hand and it slipped into the sink. It sounded like it cracked but didn't. I rinsed it again under the tap, ignoring them both.

"I have to go," Matt announced after the dishes were dried and stacked in the cupboard. Papa invited him to come over any time. He thanked Papa courteously and I walked him out. He held the door shut and we kissed in the doorway.

"Come stay with me," Matt said. "We can be ourselves there." I patted the roof of his car and watched him back out the driveway. But this is how I am around my father, I thought as he drove away. I am myself here.

Papa puttered around the house, waiting for a mah-johg call. He was so restless that I wished he would just go out, go grocery shopping, or go take a nap. I lay on the couch, watching sitcom re-runs. Strange how anyone would want to have the boring lives of TV families. Most the episodes were about the children anyway. The kids had or caused all the problems and the perfect parents helped them with a few guiding words punctuated with tearful hugs. Without the kids there would be no show.

Papa wandered in from the backyard. "You have so much time to watch TV. Lazy. Go clean you room. Take out the boxes." I yawned and stretched.

"I will."

"Now!"

"Okay, okay. I said I will."

Papa glared at me. "I can't tell you what to do? You been home one month. Every week I say move those boxes. Do you listen? It's too big a job?" I shook my head, dumbfounded.

"One month you are home. One month! Still, boxes in the house. Why? You too big to listen to one man? I'm too old to tell you what to do?"

He stormed towards the bedrooms, came back with a packing carton in his arms and dropped it on the ground. My clothes spilled onto the floor. He marched back for more. I heard the tumbling of cardboard boxes but I was too surprised to move. Back and forth he went, a furious tide throwing boxes, scattering my belongings, until he ran out of energy and disappeared down the hall, slamming his door.

The phone rang four times before Matt picked up.

"I want to leave," I croaked. My throat was dry and constricted.

He asked what was wrong and quickly suggested that I go to his place. "We'll figure this out later," he said, "just come over." I sat on my bed, hugging my duffel bag stuffed with clothes. The boxes were in the garage. Papa hasn't come out of his room. I stared at the thin, white wall and knew that he could hear me talking on the phone.

"I can't."

Matt sighed, his breath crackling in the receiver. "Do what you need to do, Peter. I'll be here."

I pushed the duffel bag away and hung up. In my rush to pack and leave, I didn't notice the sun setting. A rusty, early evening light slanted through the window splaying the shadow of a tree branch across my bed and up the wall. I'm lucky to have an escape route, I thought as I lay down on the bed and stared at the ceiling.

This is it, I'd thought as I was moving the boxes out to the garage. My chance to run, my excuse to leave. But having had some time to wait, to catch my breath and think things through, I knew it wasn't right. That's the difference between people and animals. People have instincts, yes, but reacting instinctively isn't always the best thing to do. That's why we need that extra moment to pause and choose.

A muffled rumble rolled through the wall into my room. Papa had fallen asleep. I turned on my side to face the wall and listened to the flow and ebb of his breath. The gentle rhythm pulled at me and my mind began to drift. Later, his snoring will become louder, throatier, as he'll sink deeper and deeper into sleep. Perhaps his snorting and racking cough will wake me, and I'll listen for the quiet and count the seconds, but I'll be here. I'll be here until his snoring no long shakes the walls, and then I'll run before the drowning silence fills this house.

Help Me, Help Me Not.

KIRBY HSU

Even though I've been HIV positive for a few years, it was not until three months ago that I became sick. When I say sick, I mean helplessly sick. My doctor told me that I needed a minor surgery to put a porto-cath in my chest. Similar to a permanent intravenous line, it administrates a daily medication to control an infection so I won't go blind.

I was kind of sickly growing up but I've never had any major illnesses up to this point in my life. What was supposed to be a minor day-surgery — in by 10 am and out by 2 pm — to put in this tube in my chest, turned out to be a major lesson in life.

The surgery, itself, went well enough. I was sedated and given morphine during the procedure. Except for feeling somewhat dopey in the recovery room, I felt no pain or side effects. It was after the morphine wore off that afternoon when I was home that I started to feel the impact of this "minor" surgery. The doctor had given me a prescription for Tylenol with codeine but let me assure you, it did nothing but make me dizzy and drowsy. I was in pain and no matter what I took, I was still in pain. It was a pain deeper than anything I had known. A hole had been opened up in my chest, my muscles cut apart, and a foreign object implanted and stitched into it. If I analyzed the pain, I could imagine everything that happened in the operating room and rationalize why I would feel so much P-A-I-N and why I could hardly move. All I could do was eat, watch TV, and fall asleep. This was an endless cycle for three days.

The worst thing about being helplessly sick is having to depend on people to do things for you. I was brought up to be independent. I was trained to be the new breed of "strong yet sensitive superman." I was to count on myself for everything. Not only was I successful at work, I could also cook up a storm, sew minor alterations, plant a garden, and partition a basement. I thought I had it made.

Your life changes when you have to depend on others to do things for you. I had to learn patience — major patience. It was very hard for me to ask people to do things for me. I was more used to taking care of others. But even though it was difficult, I was determined to learn. Naively, as if it should have been a surprise, I discovered that when you ask people to do things, they do it when they are ready, not when you want it. They do things their way and not your way. When you ask, you have to say please, and when they finish, even though it may not have been what you wanted, you must say thank you. To complain would be to appear ungrateful. Being dependent nearly drove me crazy.

Things also seem to take forever when you rely on people. Sometimes, by the time they got to me, I was already asleep. Other times, people came and woke me up when I did not need their help. I probably sound ungrateful but that's not what I mean.

There were times when help arrived just when I needed it. Those times felt wonderful. Let me tell you that it is not easy trying to help someone, I've had volunteer jobs. It is, however, equally difficult asking for help. I find it easier to ask my friends and close ones for help than strangers. My friends know me and my personality, they do not take offense as easily if I am in a bad mood. Because they care about me, they are more likely to take care of me even when I don't need it. They may tend to overdo it, but I understand that need. Even if it is really more for them than for me, I can still enjoy it.

I find it more difficult to ask for help from volunteers. They owe me nothing and they don't have a history with me. I don't know why they want to help or what they expect out of it. The worst part is they don't know me or my quirky habits which means I have to explain everything. Sometimes it feels like by the time I finish giving instructions, I could have done it myself.

Normally I enjoy being bossy, but under these circumstances it feels tedious. When I finally get help from a volunteer, it's my turn to feel guilty. The volunteers don't expect anything from me in return when they help me. I cannot give them anything of value except a thank-you and, wallowing in my guilt, I wonder if that's enough. I feel that I shouldn't ask for help too often since I am getting something for nothing and I certainly don't deserve that. At least that's what I've been taught to believe.

Let me stress again that I am not complaining about the help that I've gotten. It's been wonderful. People have the best intentions when they volunteer, but I have all these emotions when I am being helped and I want to share them with care-givers so we can find a way to work better together.

First, there needs to be more communication. We need to get to know each other a bit. A care team needs to get to know each other, to develop a bond and trust before a crisis develops. Both the client and the volunteer need to learn to say no without feeling rejected. The client needs to learn to ask for help and the care-giver needs to learn to ask clients if they need help. Patience goes both ways.

Even if the client says no, the caregiver needs to persevere and regularly ask what kind of help the client wants. The fact that you ask makes them feel better and, with time, they will ask you for help.

I want help when I need it. I don't want help when I don't need it. Don't decide for me what's best for me. Let me decide for myself. Sometimes, it means letting me make a mistake but I'll learn the next time. It helps me to know that I can make a mistake if that's what I choose. I truly appreciate your help so let's work together.

Sketchbook

NHAN DUC NGUYEN

The Fairy Tale of Ms Saigon

KIRBY HSU

Once upon a time in the never never land of the Mekong Delta, there lived a boy named Kim. He was quite happy until the age of fifteen when suddenly his father died. Two years after, his mother married a bully who became the wicked stepfather. This is a tale about Kim as Ms Saigon, Chris as the American soldier boy and Trung as the Vietnamese boyfriend.

Saigon — April 1975

Ms Saigon nudges up his back. He wants to take in all of this American soldier boy Chris. Legs up in the air wedged by the soldier's mighty torso, Kim admires the chiselled handsome face topped by a blond crew-cut. Firmly, he squeezes the American's bulging biceps. Over the powerful shoulders and onto the chest, his fingers glide through the fine blond hair on the armour-like pecs. He strokes with his palms the sweaty nipples making them hard and erect. With one hand, Kim breaks an ampule of poppers dispersing the musty fragrance into the humid, tropical air. He concentrates on totally giving in so as to let the soldier's big manhood inside of him. How he adores that golden cannon rod, so huge compared to his own and so rosy at its knob. The power of the soldier's thrusts sends tidal waves through his body making him weak and vulnerable. He now moves in rhythm keeping pace with the soldier's groans. One more plunge from Chris against Ms Saigon's upward nudge, it hangs in deep and still. Watching the soldier's head toss up, face crunched, Ms Saigon leans forward sucking hard on the nipples. Quivering surges come forth from deep within. Ms Saigon feels mighty and powerful knowing that he now has everything of the soldier boy inside of him.

This story begins when Kim is found out to be a homosexual by his wicked stepfather. Kim is beaten and gets kicked out of his home into the streets of Saigon. There is chaos and panic in the air. The coming of the Vietcong is rumoured to be imminent. Young and adventurous, Kim's instincts lead him to a gay bar. A number of American GIs are present. The soldiers want the Vietnamese boys to put on a drag contest. For the prize, the winner gets to pick an American soldier boy. Fresh-faced Kim wins the contest easily and is crowned Ms Saigon. Kim picks the American soldier boy Chris. They fuck for days amidst the fall of Saigon. As the city collapses and the Americans pull out, Kim and Chris vow to meet once again in the U.S. of A.

Los Angeles — April 1976

Soldier boy glides his manhood along the silky mounds of the lean muscular Vietnamese boy Trung. He thrusts against the tight opening resisting his entry. Laying down slowly on Trung's back, he gently caresses the nape of the boy's neck. He licks the smooth skin as he uses his powerful thighs to spread apart the boy's legs. Under his belly, he feels Trung's firm body squirming for his huge prick. As he senses the boy's tension easing, he presses forward, slipping inside. Arching his pelvis,

soldier boy focuses on the moist warm shaft around the head of his
golden rod. He knows it takes patience, wanting to go as deeply as he
can. Moving in slowly, he grinds his pelvis against the soft hairless
humps. His eyes shut, Trung's soft moaning flashes back to his passion
with Ms Saigon. The aroma of amyl nitrate seems to saturate the humid,
stuffy air. He feels the boy's back starting to move in rhythm to the strokes
of his prick. There is no longer any resistance. Soldier boy picks up his
pace, almost slapping his pubis against the soft submissive mounds with
each downward stroke. He plunges forward into the boy's neck, sucking
hard and biting, pain and pleasure mixing indistinguishably. He wraps his
arm around the lean smooth body possessing all that's beneath him. The
soldier boy pounds on the boy faster and faster, finally sending his mighty
and powerful slugs deep inside the Vietnamese boy.

Some time back in U.S. of A., the soldier boy cannot get over the trauma of the war.
He often gets depressed and starts drinking heavily. For his salvation, he meets a
refugee Vietnamese boy about the age of Ms Saigon. They fuck passionately and need-
ing each other, decide to live together.

In the meantime, Kim has left Vietnam. After a few months in Thailand, he makes his
way to America, ultimately settling in San Francisco. He works hard saving his money
over the years and opens a small restaurant of his own. In honour of the old country,
he names his restaurant "Ms Saigon." His business prospers and he becomes rich and
respectable. In his free time, he frequents rice bars. It's easy for him to have sex with
white guys but he has never fallen in love.

Down in L.A., soldier boy continues to drink heavily and gets into trouble often. From
time to time, he would take his frustrations out on Trung when he's drunk. The next
day, he would be very remorseful, sending flowers and gifts to make up. Trung understands Chris and tries to take good care of him. Sometimes he wants to leave but is too
afraid to try to make it on his own.

San Francisco — 1979

Ms Saigon seals his lips on those of the Vietnamese boy. Two sweaty
bodies lock in tight embrace. Their tongues intertwine, searching deeply
into each other. Their dicks rub against each other, sliding wet and hard.
Slowly Trung moves down on Ms Saigon, licking the salty sweat off his
muscular chest. Kim shifts his body around. Greedily he takes all of the
boy's prick into his mouth. He plunges right to the base, rubbing his nose
into the pubic hair. Coming up for air, he plunges down again until the rod
comfortably hits the back of his throat. The boy strokes Kim as he encircles
the hairless balls with his mouth. Trung hastens his strokes on Kim as
his own tension rises. Kim arches his pelvis, the boy instinctively puts his
mouth to the head. The shuddering shoots through both bodies, each
hungrily swallowing up the other. When the cumming stops, they lay
back feeling content and happy in each other's embrace.

Trung gets beaten by soldier boy once again. This time he leaves and is determined to
make it on his own. He goes far, far away to the fairyland of San Francisco looking for
work. At the end of the day, his fate brings him to "Ms Saigon". Kim notices the

Vietnamese boy's bruises and cuts. After Trung tells his story, Kim offers him a place to stay. They end up sleeping together. They fuck and fall in love.

For emotional support Trung brings Kim along to pick up his belongings at the soldier boy's place. Chris, in a drunk state, is surprised by the appearance of Ms Saigon. Kim, equally surprised, is willing to let Trung stay with soldier boy. He offers to help Chris get back on his feet if he tries to be good to Trung. Chris confesses that he is still in love with Ms Saigon. Kim, however, has no particular feelings for the soldier boy anymore. Chris admits there is no future for him and Trung. He confesses to a lot of shame and guilt. In the end, soldier boy goes into the other room and shoots himself. Dying in the arms of Ms Saigon, he talks of his love for the last time and pleads with Kim to take care of Trung.

* * * * *